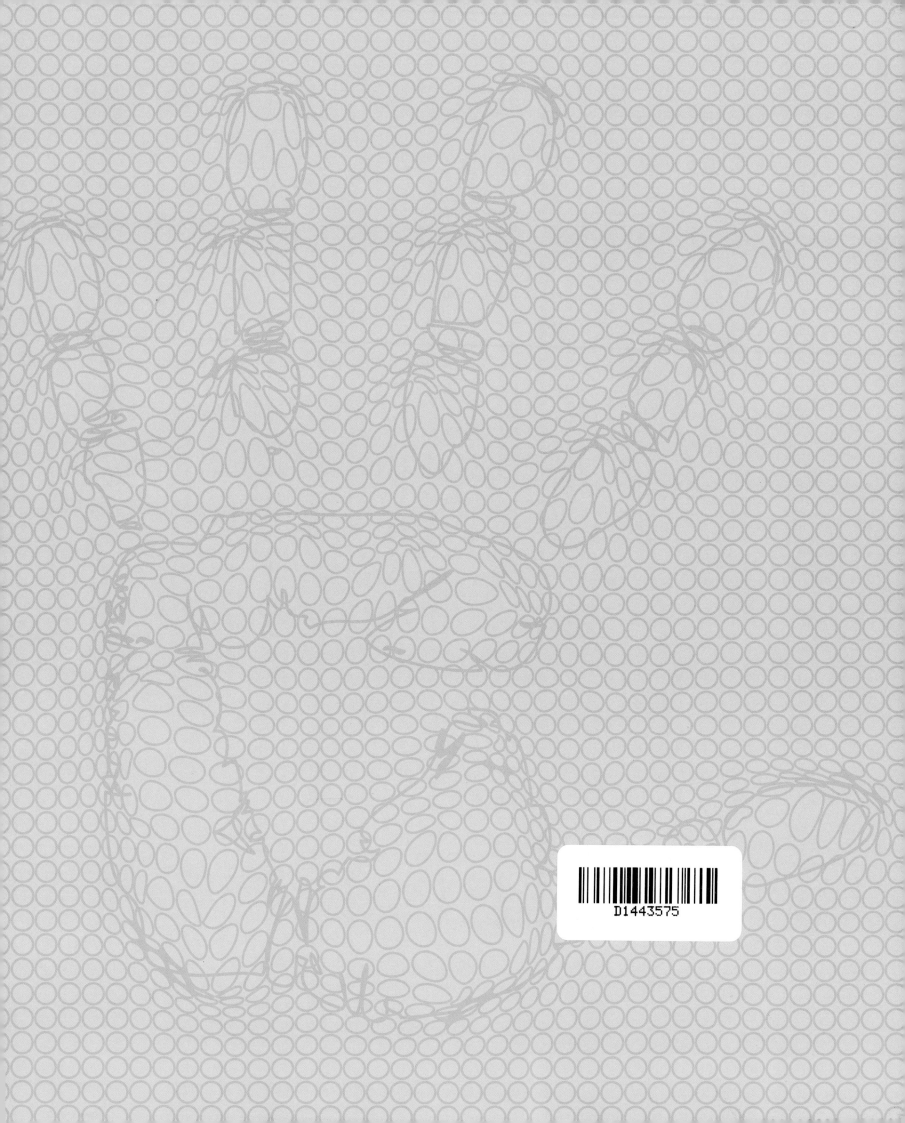

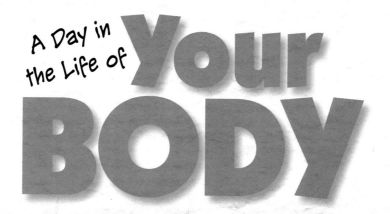

A Day in the Life of Your BODY

First edition for the United States and Canada
published in 2012 by Barron's Educational Series, Inc.

Conceived and produced by Weldon Owen Pty Ltd
59-61 Victoria Street, McMahons Point
Sydney, NSW 2060, Australia

WELDON OWEN PTY LTD
Managing Director Kay Scarlett
Publisher Corinne Roberts
Creative Director Sue Burk
Production Director Todd Rechner
Images Manager Trucie Henderson

Managing Editor Averil Moffat
Project Editor Lesley MacFadzean
Designer Karen Sagovac
Design Assistants Nathan Grice, Emily Spencer

Illustrations Argosy Publishing Inc.

All inquiries should be addressed to:
Barron's Educational Series, Inc.
250 Wireless Boulevard
Hauppauge, New York 11788
www.barronseduc.com

ISBN: 978-0-7641-6484-2

Library of Congress Control No.: 2011925562

Date of manufacture: December 2011

Manufactured by 1010 Printing International Limited,
Hui Zhou, China

The paper used in the manufacture of this book is
sourced from wood grown in sustainable forests.
It complies with the Environmental Management
System Standard ISO 14001:2004

A WELDON OWEN PRODUCTION

9 8 7 6 5 4 3 2 1

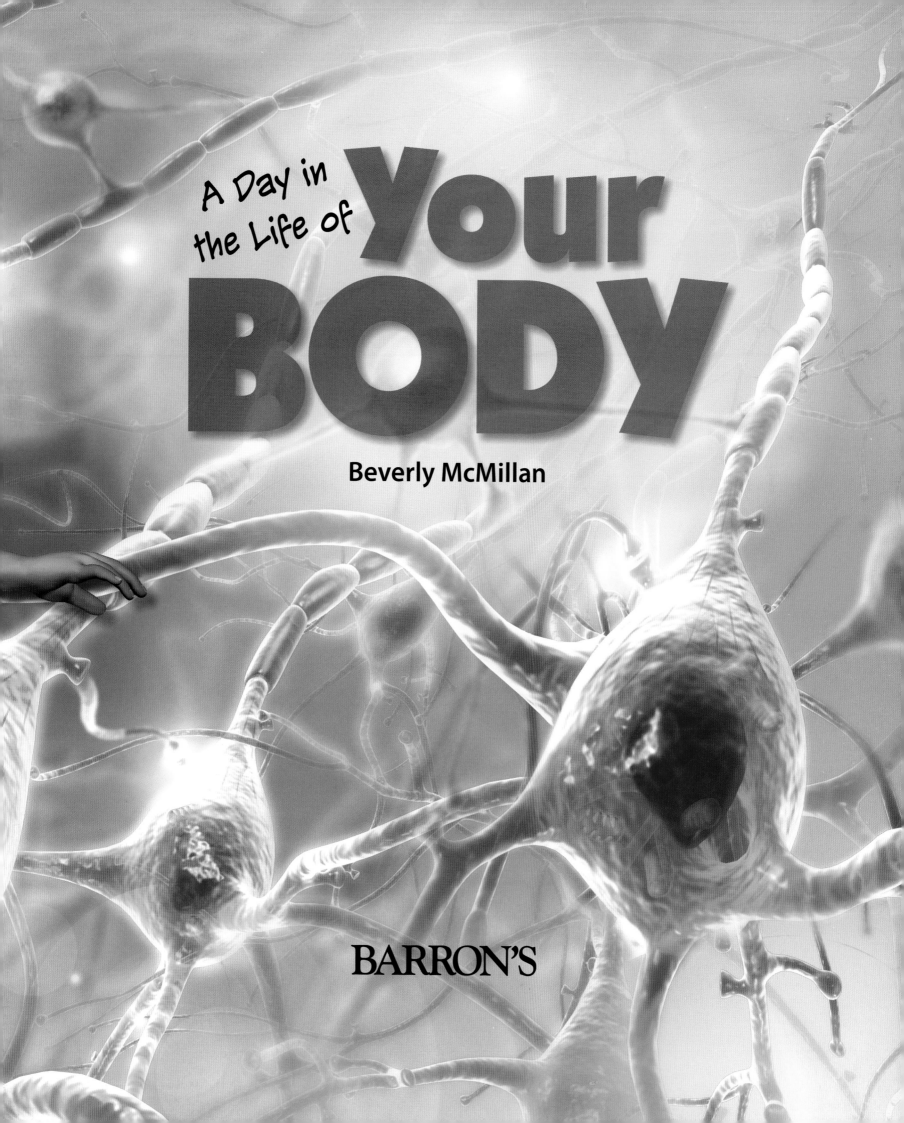

A Day in the Life of **Your BODY**

Beverly McMillan

BARRON'S

Contents

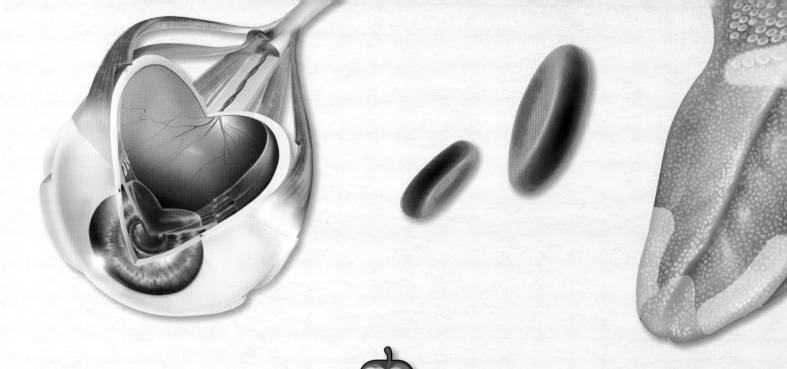

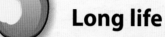

Long life

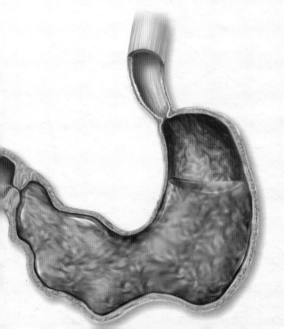

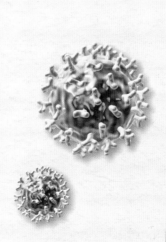

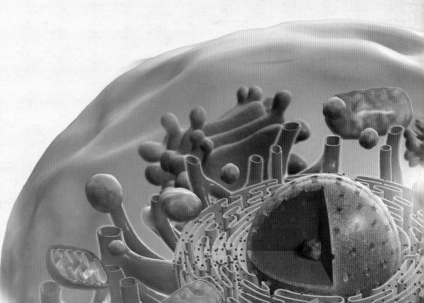

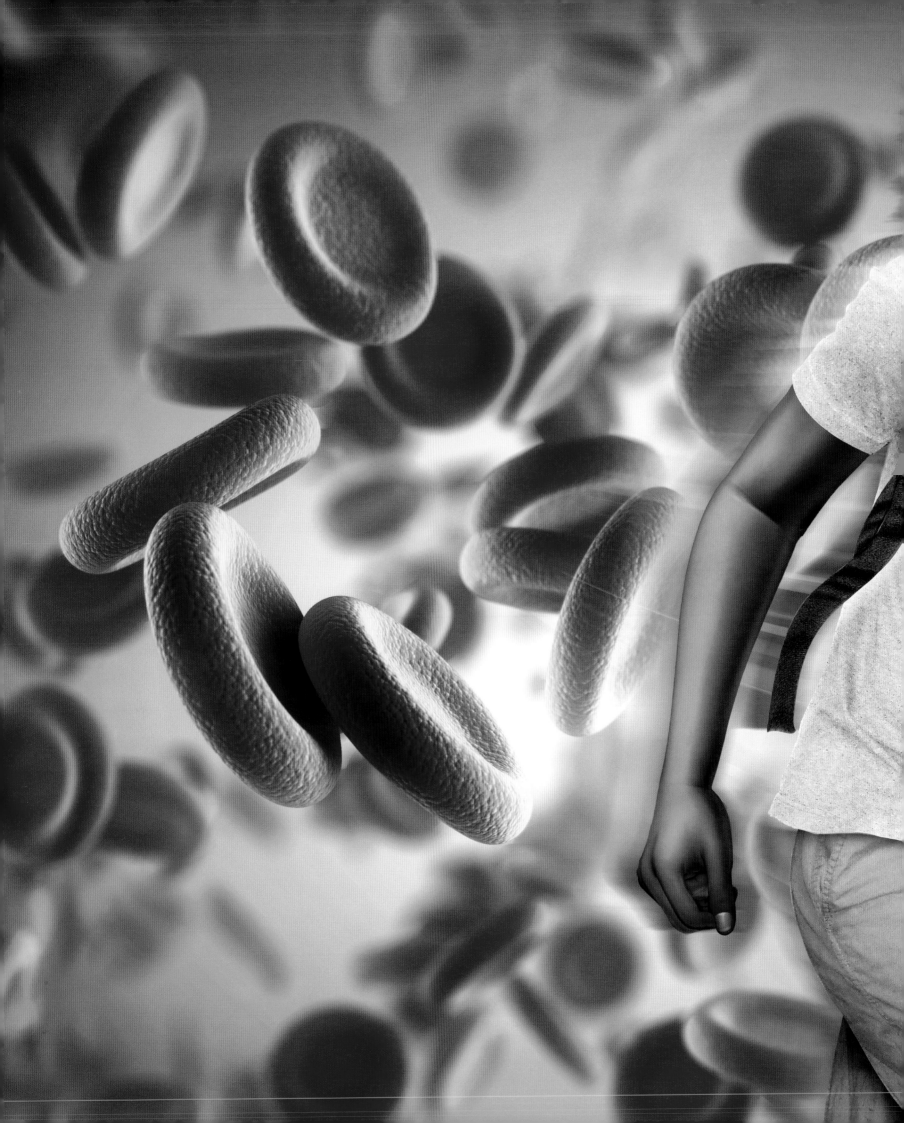

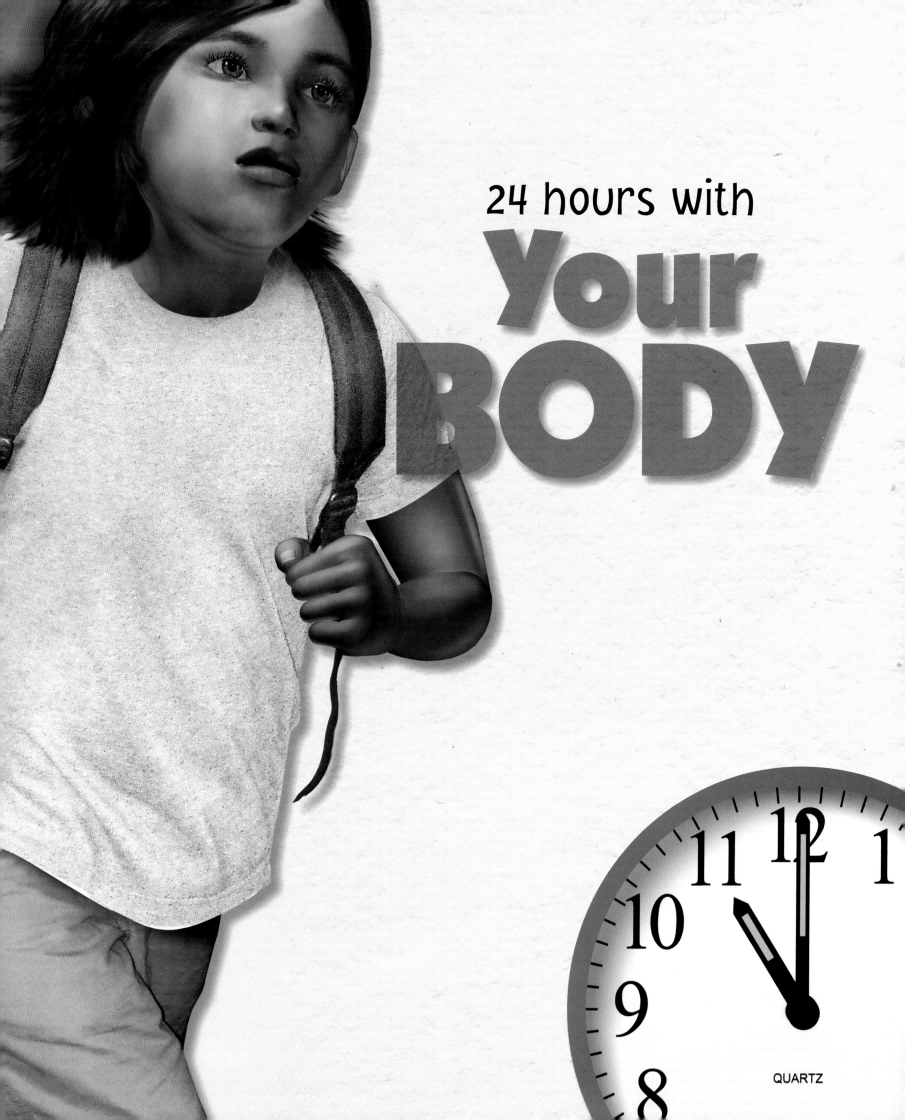

24 hours with

Your
BODY

QUARTZ

Rise and shine!

When you wake up, you become aware of the world around you, thanks to signals from your body's neurons, or nerve cells. Nerve cells in the brain and in the spinal cord, running down your spine, form the central nervous system. Long cable-like extensions of nerve cells are bundled into nerves. They run through the rest of your body and form the peripheral nervous system. Nerves bring information from your eyes and other sense organs to the brain. They also carry orders from the brain and spinal cord to your muscles and internal organs. Your endocrine system makes chemicals called hormones that work with the brain to control many functions.

Brain during
sleep

Waking the brain

Brain scans provide an amazing window into how the brain works. Some parts of the brain are most active when you are asleep while others shift into higher gear as you wake up. A ringing alarm clock or sun streaming in a window is a signal for the brain to begin managing the physical and mental activity that will get you through your day.

Brain when
awake

A signal pathway

Many body activities are controlled by signals passed by three types of nerve cells. Sensory neurons pick up information from sense organs, such as the eyes and ears. Their messages travel to inter-neurons in the spinal cord or brain. Inter-neurons process the information and may then signal motor neurons, which command your muscles.

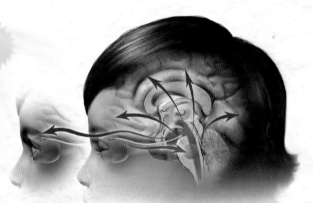

Eyes open and closed
Light shining through your eyelids reaches the brain, which sends signals that open your eyes.

Chemical messengers

A chemical called a neurotransmitter carries the message from a nerve cell to a receiving cell. When the chemical reaches a receiver, such as a muscle cell, the cell's activity changes.

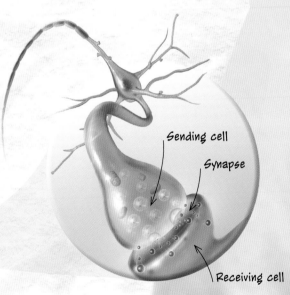

Sending cell

Synapse

Receiving cell

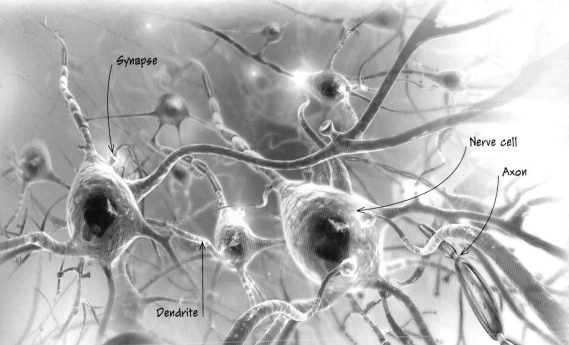

Synapse

Nerve cell

Axon

Dendrite

Nerve cells communicate

A nerve cell's outgoing signals speed down a threadlike axon. A receiving nerve cell picks up the message by way of short, spiky projections called dendrites. The space where an axon sends its signals to dendrites is called a synapse.

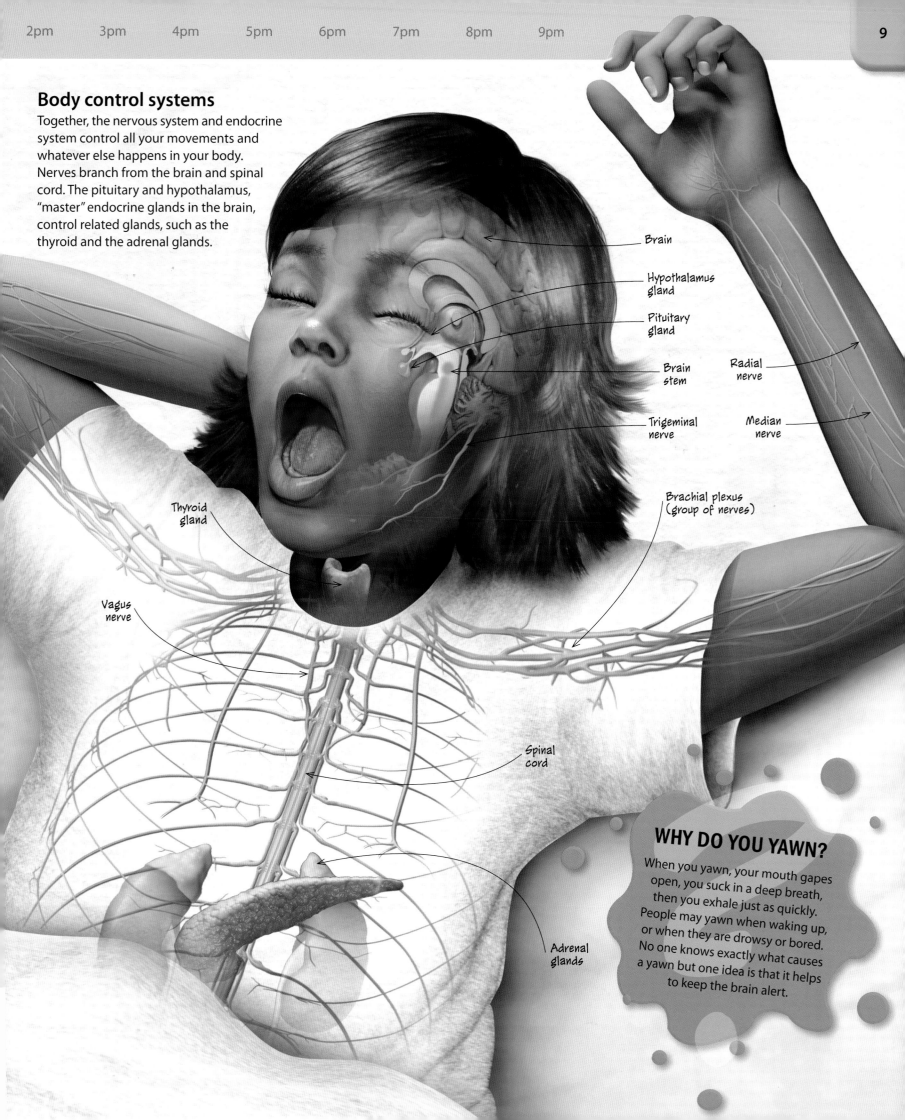

Body control systems

Together, the nervous system and endocrine system control all your movements and whatever else happens in your body. Nerves branch from the brain and spinal cord. The pituitary and hypothalamus, "master" endocrine glands in the brain, control related glands, such as the thyroid and the adrenal glands.

Brain

Hypothalamus gland

Pituitary gland

Brain stem

Trigeminal nerve

Radial nerve

Median nerve

Brachial plexus (group of nerves)

Thyroid gland

Vagus nerve

Spinal cord

Adrenal glands

WHY DO YOU YAWN?

When you yawn, your mouth gapes open, you suck in a deep breath, then you exhale just as quickly. People may yawn when waking up, or when they are drowsy or bored. No one knows exactly what causes a yawn but one idea is that it helps to keep the brain alert.

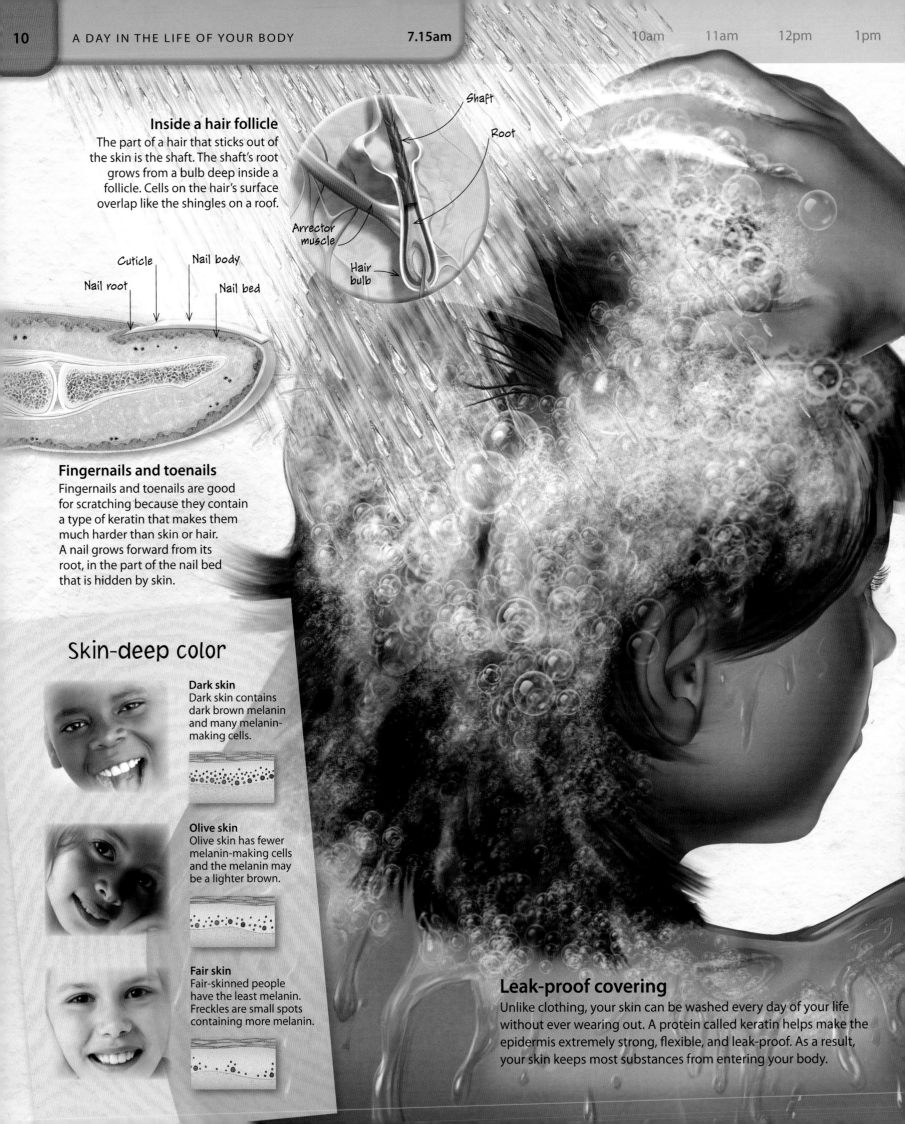

Inside a hair follicle

The part of a hair that sticks out of the skin is the shaft. The shaft's root grows from a bulb deep inside a follicle. Cells on the hair's surface overlap like the shingles on a roof.

Shaft

Root

Arrector muscle

Hair bulb

Cuticle

Nail body

Nail root

Nail bed

Fingernails and toenails

Fingernails and toenails are good for scratching because they contain a type of keratin that makes them much harder than skin or hair. A nail grows forward from its root, in the part of the nail bed that is hidden by skin.

Skin-deep color

Dark skin
Dark skin contains dark brown melanin and many melanin-making cells.

Olive skin
Olive skin has fewer melanin-making cells and the melanin may be a lighter brown.

Fair skin
Fair-skinned people have the least melanin. Freckles are small spots containing more melanin.

Leak-proof covering

Unlike clothing, your skin can be washed every day of your life without ever wearing out. A protein called keratin helps make the epidermis extremely strong, flexible, and leak-proof. As a result, your skin keeps most substances from entering your body.

A good head of hair
If you are like most people, you have about 100,000 hairs on your scalp, similar to the two hairs shown here. Your scalp probably sheds about 25 to 100 hairs every day but new hairs are growing to replace them.

New skin from old
This microscope photograph shows dead cells at the surface of the skin. Now ready to fall off, the cells have been pushed upward as new skin cells form beneath them. This renewal cycle takes about six weeks.

Shower and shampoo

When you soap up in the shower, you are cleaning your body's largest organ—the skin. Your skin weighs about 9 pounds (4 kg) and, with your hair and nails, it makes up your integumentary system. The skin has two layers and, over most of your body, it is about as thick as a sheet of paper. The outer layer is the epidermis. Beneath it is the dermis, which is laced with blood vessels and with nerve endings that provide your sense of touch. Hair follicles and glands that release oil or sweat thread through the epidermis to the outside. The epidermis also contains cells that fight microbes. Curving ridges on the surface of the epidermis make your fingerprints another of your skin's special features.

Oil
(sebaceous)
gland

Sweat
gland

Nerve

Dermis

Epidermis

Blood
vessels

Skin clogs and pimples

Having pimples is a natural part of growing up. A blackhead forms when the opening of an oil gland clogs up. Infection by bacteria can cause a pimple that contains pus. This condition is called acne. Antibiotics can help to clear it up.

Acne
Acne can develop on the face, back, and upper chest.

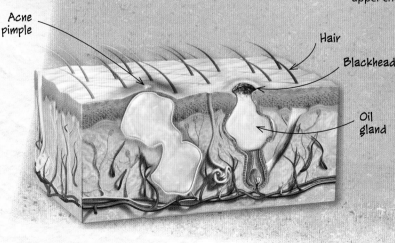

Acne
pimple

Hair

Blackhead

Oil
gland

Clothes hanger

When you get dressed, you are hanging your clothes on your body's sturdy framework— its skeletal system of bones and cartilage. Your skeleton consists of about 206 bones that support your body's flesh and protect soft internal organs. For example, your ribs protect your heart and lungs; skull bones protect your brain. The ends of some bones and the vertebrae that make up your spine are cushioned by rubbery cartilage. For as long as you live, your bones are renewed as newly formed bone replaces older bone. If you break a bone, this renewal process heals the injury.

Holding it together
Without connective tissues, your skeleton would be a heap of separate bones. There are several kinds of these "connector" tissues. Ligaments attach bones to one another. Tendons connect bones to muscles. Cartilage is another type of connective tissue.

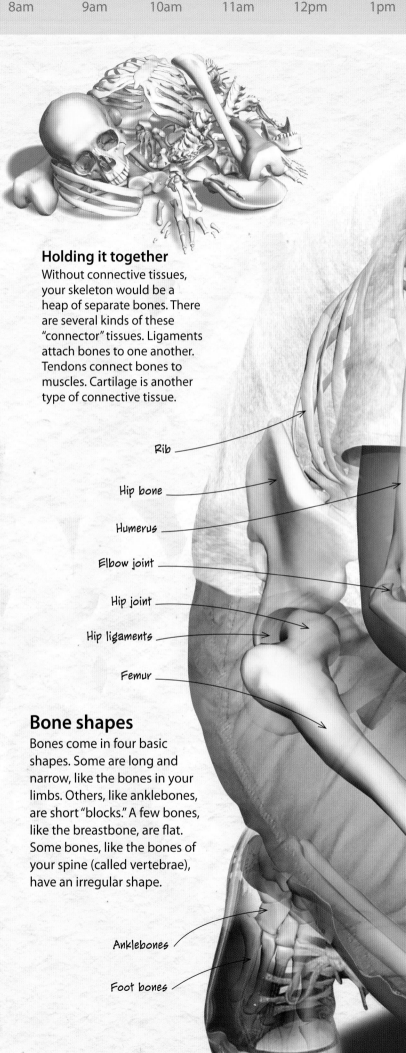

Rib

Hip bone

Humerus

Elbow joint

Hip joint

Hip ligaments

Femur

Bone shapes
Bones come in four basic shapes. Some are long and narrow, like the bones in your limbs. Others, like anklebones, are short "blocks." A few bones, like the breastbone, are flat. Some bones, like the bones of your spine (called vertebrae), have an irregular shape.

Anklebones

Foot bones

Movable joints

A joint is where two or more bones come together. Some joints allow bones to move. In movable joints a bone may pivot, glide, swing like a hinge, rotate like a ball in a socket, or tip or roll back and forth.

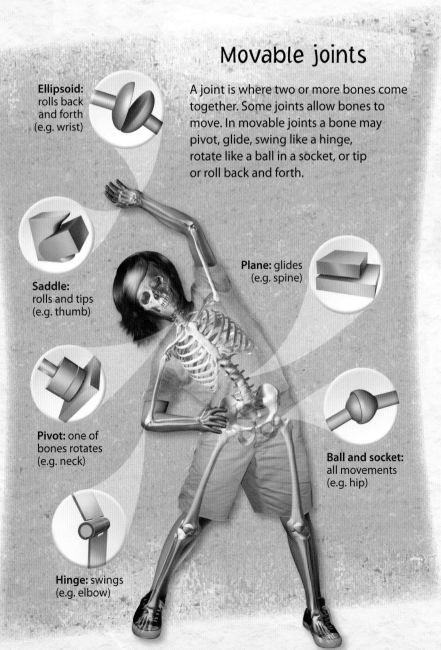

Ellipsoid: rolls back and forth (e.g. wrist)

Saddle: rolls and tips (e.g. thumb)

Plane: glides (e.g. spine)

Pivot: one of bones rotates (e.g. neck)

Ball and socket: all movements (e.g. hip)

Hinge: swings (e.g. elbow)

Stretchy ligaments

Ligaments are strong but stretchy. In the hip joint, they help hold the hip bone and thighbone together. They also help to keep your hip joints stable.

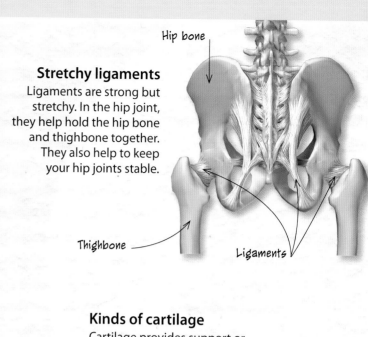

Hip bone

Thighbone

Ligaments

Vertebra

Shoulder joint

Clavicle

Breastbone

Rib cartilage

Patella

Kinds of cartilage

Cartilage provides support or padding in many parts of the skeletal system. It makes your outer ear flaps firm but bendable. Strong cartilage padding, in your knees and between the vertebrae of your spine, cushions the bones and helps them move smoothly.

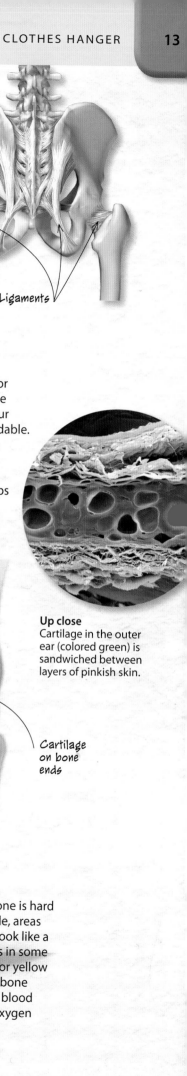

Spongy bone

Red marrow

Compact bone

Yellow marrow

Tibia

Wrist bones

Thighbone

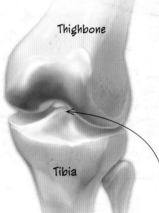

Tibia

Cartilage on bone ends

Up close

Cartilage in the outer ear (colored green) is sandwiched between layers of pinkish skin.

Inside a bone

The outside of a bone is hard and compact. Inside, areas with open spaces look like a sponge. The spaces in some bones contain red or yellow bone marrow. Red bone marrow makes red blood cells, which carry oxygen in your body.

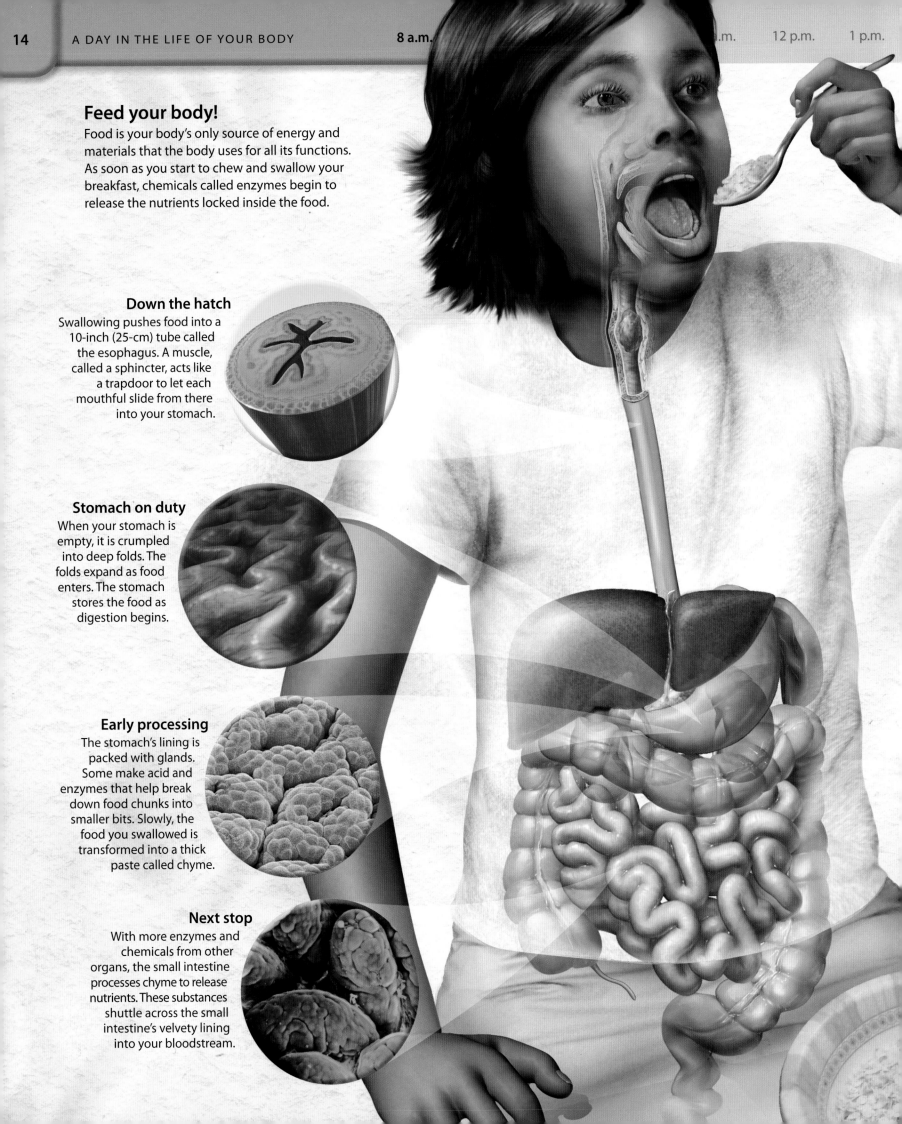

Feed your body!

Food is your body's only source of energy and materials that the body uses for all its functions. As soon as you start to chew and swallow your breakfast, chemicals called enzymes begin to release the nutrients locked inside the food.

Down the hatch

Swallowing pushes food into a 10-inch (25-cm) tube called the esophagus. A muscle, called a sphincter, acts like a trapdoor to let each mouthful slide from there into your stomach.

Stomach on duty

When your stomach is empty, it is crumpled into deep folds. The folds expand as food enters. The stomach stores the food as digestion begins.

Early processing

The stomach's lining is packed with glands. Some make acid and enzymes that help break down food chunks into smaller bits. Slowly, the food you swallowed is transformed into a thick paste called chyme.

Next stop

With more enzymes and chemicals from other organs, the small intestine processes chyme to release nutrients. These substances shuttle across the small intestine's velvety lining into your bloodstream.

Break your fast

When you eat, your digestive system swings into action to obtain nourishing substances from your food. Your mouth, teeth, stomach, and intestines are all parts of this system. Organs such as your liver, gallbladder, and pancreas help with food processing. It takes about four hours for a meal to move through the digestive tract. During this time, your body obtains the proteins, fats, sugars, vitamins, and minerals it needs.

Salivary glands

Salivary glands in your mouth produce more than a quart (1 L) of watery saliva each day. Saliva moistens food that you are chewing and has some food-digesting enzymes.

Up and out

Vomiting is one way your body gets rid of material that irritates your stomach or intestines. If you load your stomach with too much food or get a stomach "bug," your brain signals nearby muscles to spew chyme in your stomach back up through your esophagus and throat and out through your mouth.

Yucky vomit
Vomit burns your throat because chyme contains powerful stomach acid.

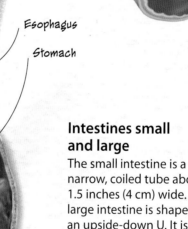

Esophagus

Stomach

Sphincter

Chyme

Small intestine

Large intestine

Intestines small and large

The small intestine is a narrow, coiled tube about 1.5 inches (4 cm) wide. The large intestine is shaped like an upside-down U. It is much shorter but wider—about 2.5 inches (7 cm) in diameter.

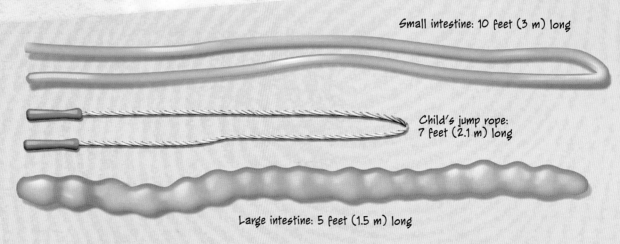

Small intestine: 10 feet (3 m) long

In with nutrients
Because the small intestine is narrow, nutrients easily reach its lining and cross into the bloodstream.

Child's jump rope: 7 feet (2.1 m) long

Out with leftovers
The short, wide large intestine stores the leftovers of food digestion and eventually expels them in bowel movements.

Large intestine: 5 feet (1.5 m) long

I'm late! I'm late!

When you are running to catch a bus, blood is racing through your body from head to toe. In fact, whatever you do, your heart and blood vessels—your circulatory system— constantly move blood to all parts of your body. The heart is a powerful muscle that pumps blood. Blood vessels are tubes that transport blood away from the heart and back again. Blood itself is a "river of life." It delivers nutrients from food and carries away wastes. Red blood cells bring oxygen to body tissues, and white blood cells fight disease. Platelets in blood help to stop the bleeding when a blood vessel is cut or torn.

Blood pressure

The heart's strong pumping pushes blood through the miles of blood vessels in your body. This flowing blood presses against the vessel walls. A blood pressure check measures the amount of pressure on these walls.

Where blood goes

One branch of your circulatory system carries blood from the right half of the heart to the lungs, where it picks up oxygen you have breathed in. This blood then flows into the left half of the heart, which pumps it out to other parts of the body.

Seeing a heartbeat

Electrical signals from a natural "pacemaker" make your heart beat. An electrocardiogram, or EKG, records these signals. The test is used to detect heart damage or to confirm that the heart is working normally. Patches that detect electricity are placed on the patient's body. An EKG is painless and takes only a few minutes.

"Reading" an EKG
The pattern of spikes and dips on an EKG show the heart's activity.

Hooked up
A child may have an EKG when a doctor suspects a problem with a heart valve or the heart's pacemaker.

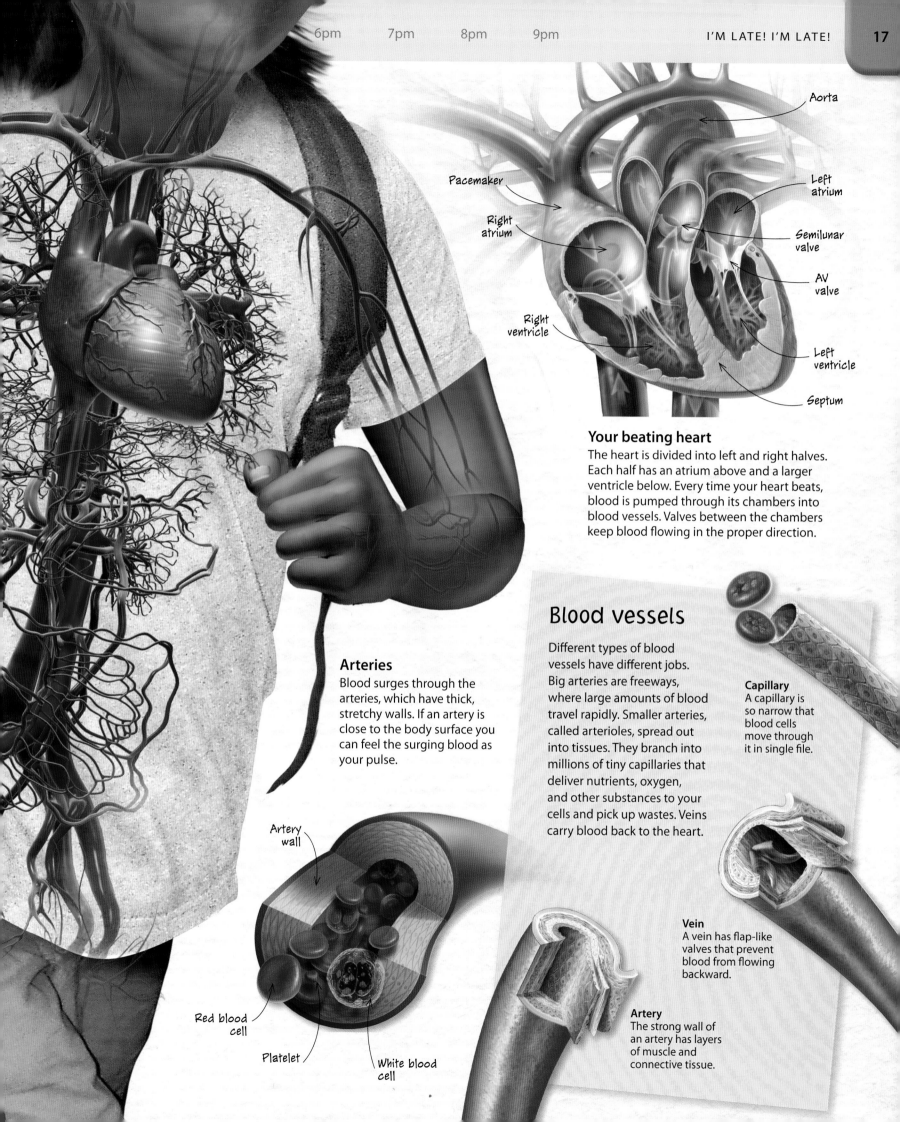

Aorta

Pacemaker

Left atrium

Right atrium

Semilunar valve

AV valve

Right ventricle

Left ventricle

Septum

Your beating heart

The heart is divided into left and right halves. Each half has an atrium above and a larger ventricle below. Every time your heart beats, blood is pumped through its chambers into blood vessels. Valves between the chambers keep blood flowing in the proper direction.

Blood vessels

Different types of blood vessels have different jobs. Big arteries are freeways, where large amounts of blood travel rapidly. Smaller arteries, called arterioles, spread out into tissues. They branch into millions of tiny capillaries that deliver nutrients, oxygen, and other substances to your cells and pick up wastes. Veins carry blood back to the heart.

Capillary
A capillary is so narrow that blood cells move through it in single file.

Vein
A vein has flap-like valves that prevent blood from flowing backward.

Arteries

Blood surges through the arteries, which have thick, stretchy walls. If an artery is close to the body surface you can feel the surging blood as your pulse.

Artery wall

Red blood cell

Platelet

White blood cell

Artery
The strong wall of an artery has layers of muscle and connective tissue.

Think! Think!

When it's test time at school, you rely on the remarkable ability of your brain to process and store information. More than 80 percent of your brain is a region called the cerebrum, which looks a little like a shelled walnut. Impulses from its billions of nerve cells allow you to think, learn, and remember. The cerebrum also manages abilities such as speaking and writing and sends the orders to muscles when you move some part of your body. Behind and below the cerebrum, the cerebellum helps control movements and balance. The brain stem connects your brain to the spinal cord. It has several important parts that manage the operations of many internal organs, such as your heart and lungs.

Hemispheres in action

The cerebrum's two hemispheres work together on most tasks but, for some "brain work," they divide the labor. In most people, the left hemisphere manages math, language skills, and logical thinking. The right hemisphere handles emotions, and artistic and musical skills. Each hemisphere controls the opposite side of the body. For example, when you move your left leg, the command for this action comes from the right cerebral hemisphere.

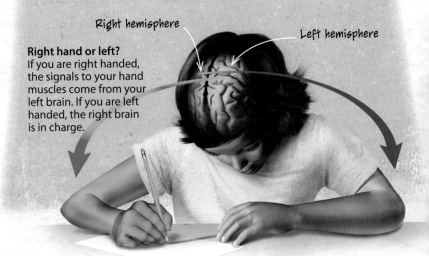

Right hand or left?
If you are right handed, the signals to your hand muscles come from your left brain. If you are left handed, the right brain is in charge.

Right hemisphere

Left hemisphere

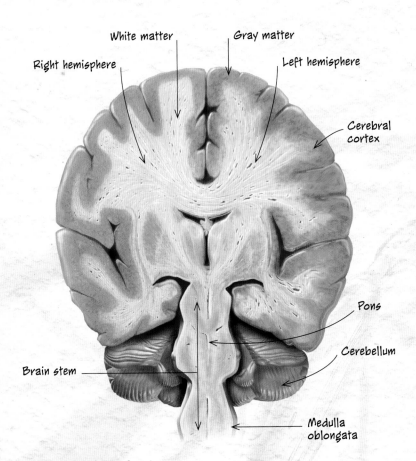

White matter

Gray matter

Right hemisphere

Left hemisphere

Cerebral cortex

Pons

Cerebellum

Brain stem

Medulla oblongata

Your thinking brain

Your cerebrum is divided into right and left halves, called hemispheres. The cerebrum's top layer, the cerebral cortex, is the center for the brain's most complex operations, like solving problems. The bodies of cerebral cortex nerve cells form gray matter. Axons form white matter.

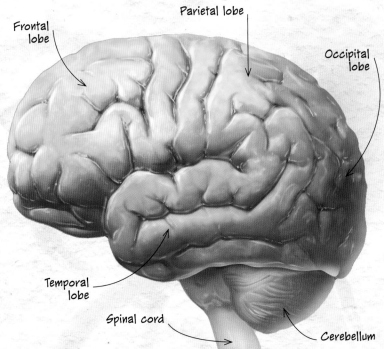

Parietal lobe

Frontal lobe

Occipital lobe

Temporal lobe

Spinal cord

Cerebellum

Brain lobes

Each half of the cerebrum is divided into regions called lobes. The frontal lobe is concerned with speaking and deliberate movements. The temporal lobe processes hearing and, together with the occipital lobe, it manages vision. The parietal lobe deals with other senses.

Learning, memory, and emotions

When you learn a fact, remember it, or need to make a decision, your cerebrum's limbic system is active. These parts loop around the brain stem and "talk" constantly with other brain areas. The limbic system is also in charge of emotions.

Subtraction

How your brain does math

You use different parts of your cerebral cortex to solve different kinds of math problems. The orange parts on these brain scans show the most active areas when someone is doing subtraction problems and those that are most active when the person is saying multiplication tables.

Amygdala
Signals related to emotions happen here and in the cingulate gyrus.

Hypothalamus
Parts of this tiny structure monitor internal organs and make you aware of being hungry or thirsty.

Cingulate gyrus

Thalamus
Signals from your eyes and other senses pass through here for processing in the cerebrum.

Pons
This brain stem area directs signals between the cerebellum and the cerebral cortex.

Hippocampus
Activity here helps your brain store memories.

Multiplication tables

Medulla oblongata
Nerve cells here control automatic functions, like breathing.

Cerebellum
Movements, balance, and the dexterity for tasks like typing on a keyboard are coordinated here.

Brain stem

WHY DO PALMS SWEAT?

Hot weather can make you sweat and so can your emotions. The limbic system is the culprit. When you feel nervous or anxious about a school test, your limbic system may send signals that boost the activity of sweat glands.

Sweat glands

Sweaty palms
The palms of your hands are well sprinkled with sweat glands.

Hang on and climb

In the gym, your skeletal muscles work hard. Most of these muscles attach to your skeleton's bones. Together they are called the muscular system. A muscle can get shorter and then longer again. This is what happens when a muscle contracts and relaxes. When a skeletal muscle contracts it pulls on a bone or a firm area of skin. Movements like tapping your fingers and toes use only a little muscle strength. When you pull yourself up a wall, however, your muscles produce much more power. Some of your largest muscles are in your back. In addition to helping you throw a ball or lift a heavy weight, they also help to support your head and upper body when you stand or sit.

Mighty muscles

You have more than 640 skeletal muscles and they come in a variety of shapes and sizes. Usually, tendons attach a skeletal muscle to at least two bones.

Quadriceps femoris

Sternocleidomastoid

Interossei

Extensor digitorum

Brachioradialis

Biceps brachii

Deltoid

Trapezius

Rhomboid

Latissimus dorsi

Working together

Skeletal muscles usually work in pairs to move a body part. For example, the biceps and triceps in your upper arm work together when you lift something or put it down.

Arm straight
When your arm straightens out, the triceps contracts and the biceps relaxes.

Relaxed biceps

Triceps brachii

Contracting triceps

Arm bent
When your arm bends, the biceps contracts and the triceps relaxes.

Contracting biceps

Relaxed triceps

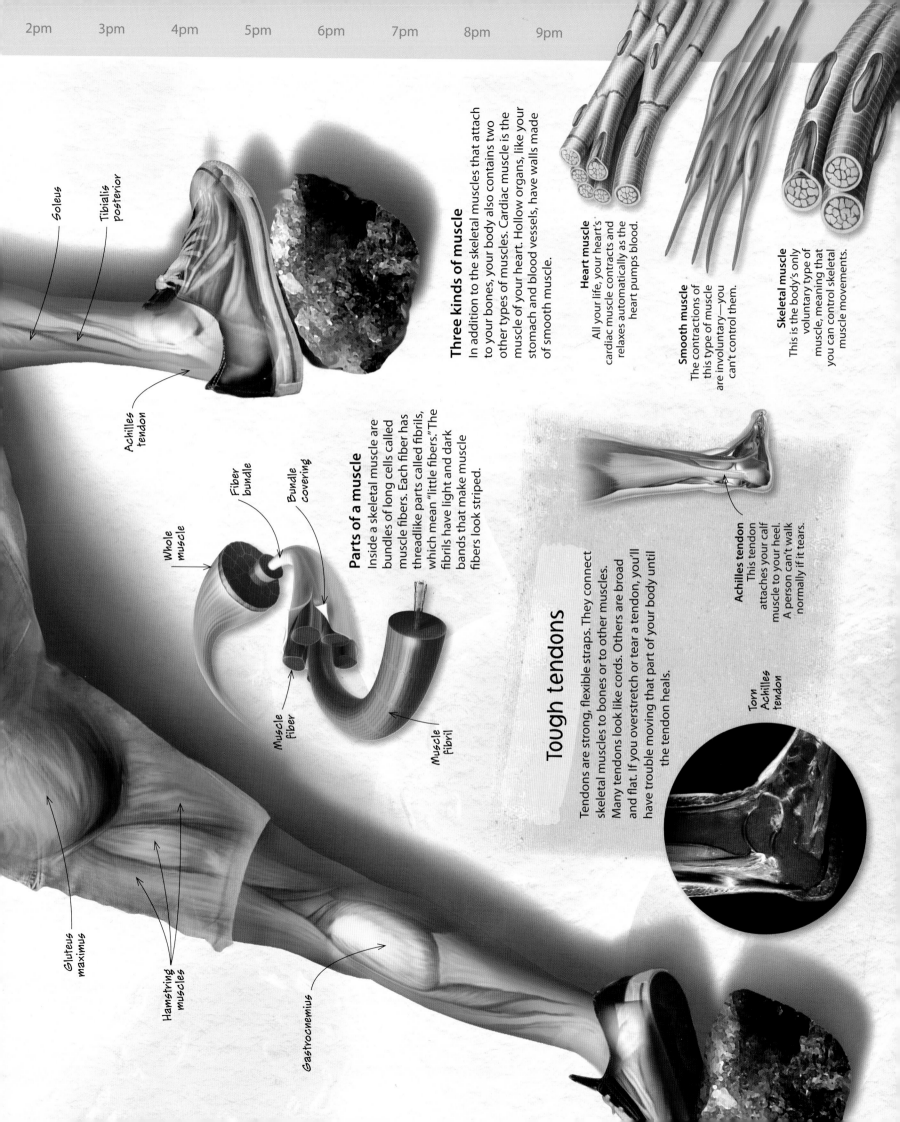

Soleus

Tibialis posterior

Achilles tendon

Three kinds of muscle

In addition to the skeletal muscles that attach to your bones, your body also contains two other types of muscles. Cardiac muscle is the muscle of your heart. Hollow organs, like your stomach and blood vessels, have walls made of smooth muscle.

Heart muscle
All your life, your heart's cardiac muscle contracts and relaxes automatically as the heart pumps blood.

Smooth muscle
The contractions of this type of muscle are involuntary—you can't control them.

Skeletal muscle
This is the body's only voluntary type of muscle, meaning that you can control skeletal muscle movements.

Whole muscle

Fiber bundle

Bundle covering

Parts of a muscle

Inside a skeletal muscle are bundles of long cells called muscle fibers. Each fiber has threadlike parts called fibrils, which mean "little fibers." The fibrils have light and dark bands that make muscle fibers look striped.

Muscle fiber

Muscle fibril

Tough tendons

Tendons are strong, flexible straps. They connect skeletal muscles to bones or to other muscles. Many tendons look like cords. Others are broad and flat. If you overstretch or tear a tendon, you'll have trouble moving that part of your body until the tendon heals.

Achilles tendon
This tendon attaches your calf muscle to your heel. A person can't walk normally if it tears.

Torn Achilles tendon

Gluteus maximus

Hamstring muscles

Gastrocnemius

Air in, air out

When you breathe, your respiratory system moves air into and out of your lungs. You can use the stream of air to sing in the school choir but its main job in the body is more important. Air contains oxygen that your body cells need to make energy. Breathing brings in oxygen for cells and removes carbon dioxide, a waste that cells make as they produce energy. When you breathe in, air rushes down to your lungs, which are located in your chest on either side of your heart. They are stretchy, so they can inflate with air a bit like a balloon. Your ribs wrap around and protect your lungs. A sheet of muscle called the diaphragm supports them from below.

Breathing in and out

Automatic signals from your brain trigger muscle movements that expand your lungs so that air flows in. Air goes into your nose or mouth, then down your throat and trachea, or windpipe. The trachea splits into tubes called bronchi, which branch into smaller tubes called bronchioles.

Inhalation   Exhalation

Nasal cavity

Pharynx

Larynx

Trachea (windpipe)

Lung

Diaphragm

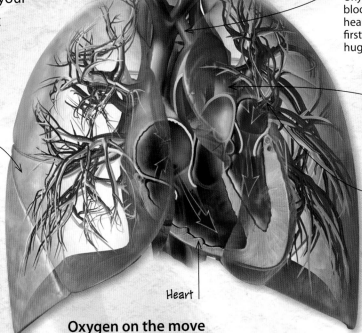

Aorta
Oxygen-rich blood from the heart is pumped first into this huge artery.

Pulmonary arteries
These large vessels carry blood to the lungs to pick up oxygen.

Pulmonary veins
These vessels return oxygen-loaded blood to the heart.

Lung

Heart

Oxygen on the move

The heart's right half pumps blood that is low in oxygen to the lungs. When it is loaded with a fresh oxygen supply, the blood moves back to the heart's left half, which pumps it out to body tissues.

Inhale, exhale

When you inhale or breathe in, the diaphragm muscle under your lungs flattens out. This expands the lungs and they suck in air. When you exhale, the diaphragm relaxes into a dome. Your lungs shrink, forcing air out.

A breathing challenge

Asthma can be a scary health problem. Airways swell up, leaving less room for air. Thick mucus may clog the narrow space, and airway muscles may squeeze the airways like fists. When all these things happen, breathing can be very difficult. An allergy or stress can trigger an attack. Inhaling a mist of medicine can unblock airways.

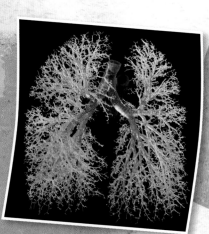

Airways and asthma
Air flows best through wide-open bronchioles.

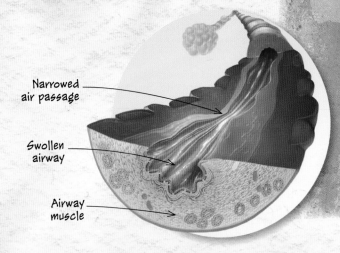

Narrowed air passage

Swollen airway

Airway muscle

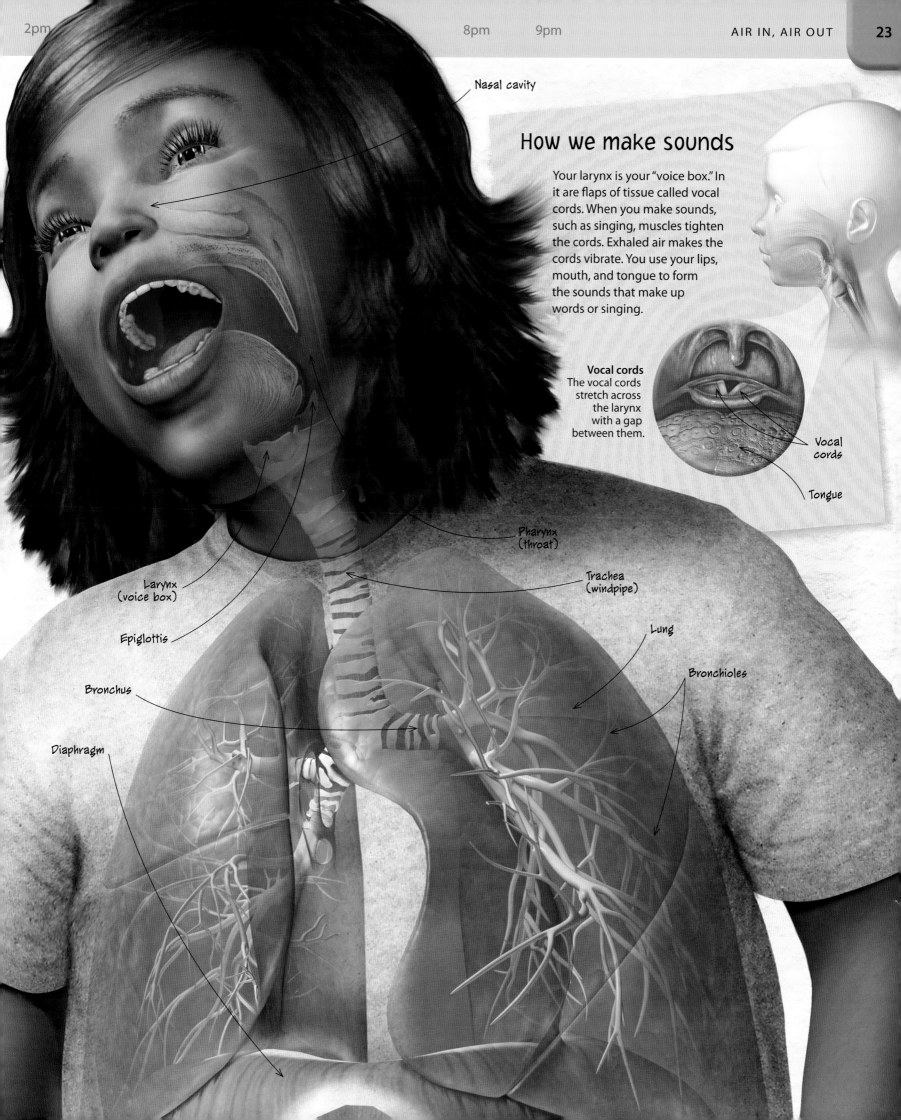

Nasal cavity

How we make sounds

Your larynx is your "voice box." In it are flaps of tissue called vocal cords. When you make sounds, such as singing, muscles tighten the cords. Exhaled air makes the cords vibrate. You use your lips, mouth, and tongue to form the sounds that make up words or singing.

Vocal cords
The vocal cords stretch across the larynx with a gap between them.

Vocal cords

Tongue

Pharynx (throat)

Larynx (voice box)

Trachea (windpipe)

Epiglottis

Lung

Bronchioles

Bronchus

Diaphragm

Sniff and sample

At lunchtime, your senses of taste and smell signal your brain about the food you eat. With both these senses, special nerve endings act as sensors that detect chemicals. Your saliva picks up chemicals in the food you are chewing and carries the chemicals to taste sensors inside your 10,000 taste buds. Patches with millions of smell sensors—called olfactory receptors—are scattered far up inside your nose. They are nerve endings that sense chemicals in air. Sharp senses of taste and smell can help us to avoid potentially harmful substances, such as food that is spoiled. In fact, we don't taste food properly unless both taste and smell sensors are operating. That is why food doesn't taste as good when your nose is stopped up with a cold.

How good is your nose?

Experts think that we humans have about 10 million smell receptors. This may seem like a lot but many other animals are much better "smellers." Rabbits and mice have at least ten times more smell receptors, and dogs are smell champions, with about 220 million. This means that dogs can tell the difference between similar smells more easily than we can.

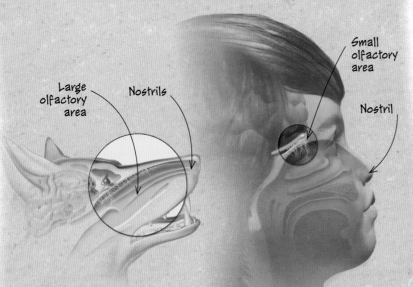

Keen smeller
The lining of a dog's nose is sprinkled with many millions of smell receptors.

Poor smeller
A human nose has far fewer smell receptors, in small patches of the upper nose lining.

Large olfactory area

Nostrils

Small olfactory area

Nostril

Taste and smell signals

Signals from taste sensors travel to the brain's taste centers. Smell receptors send their messages to the brain's olfactory bulbs. After more processing there, you become aware of the smells.

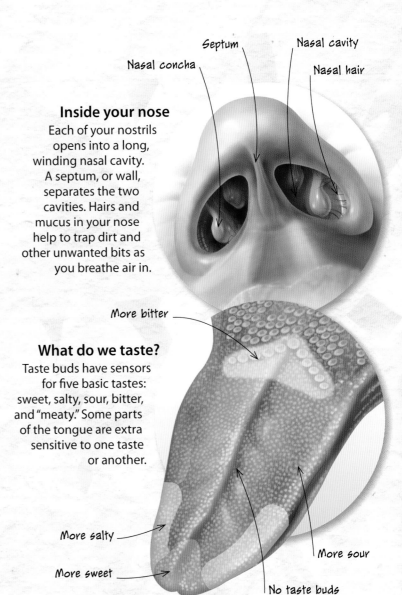

Nasal concha

Septum

Nasal cavity

Nasal hair

Inside your nose

Each of your nostrils opens into a long, winding nasal cavity. A septum, or wall, separates the two cavities. Hairs and mucus in your nose help to trap dirt and other unwanted bits as you breathe air in.

More bitter

What do we taste?

Taste buds have sensors for five basic tastes: sweet, salty, sour, bitter, and "meaty." Some parts of the tongue are extra sensitive to one taste or another.

More salty

More sour

More sweet

No taste buds

Where are taste buds?

Taste buds are tucked down inside flat bumps on your tongue called papillae, which look like tiny cushions. Saliva washes chemicals in food down to them. Taste buds wear out and, in young people, they are replaced about every two weeks.

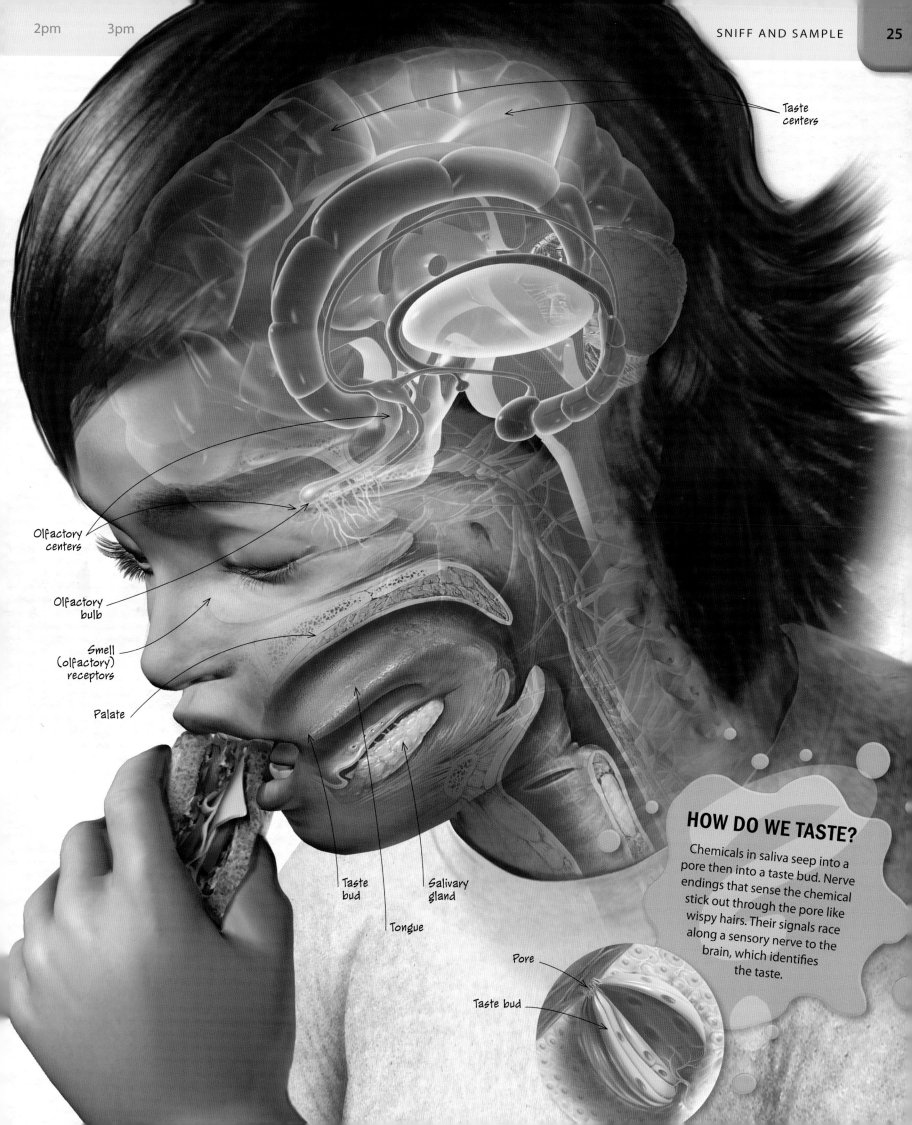

Taste centers

Olfactory centers

Olfactory bulb

Smell (olfactory) receptors

Palate

Taste bud

Tongue

Salivary gland

HOW DO WE TASTE?

Chemicals in saliva seep into a pore then into a taste bud. Nerve endings that sense the chemical stick out through the pore like wispy hairs. Their signals race along a sensory nerve to the brain, which identifies the taste.

Pore

Taste bud

Listen up . . . don't wobble

Your ears are tools for two important tasks—hearing sounds and keeping your balance. The three parts of an ear—called the outer, middle, and inner ear—all help to pick up sounds in the world around us. A sound is vibrating air that moves in waves. When the waves reach sensors in a part of the inner ear called the cochlea, a nerve sends signals to the brain. The brain uses these signals to rework the sound waves into the sense we call hearing. The inner ear also contains looping tubes filled with fluid and sacs that hold tiny "ear stones." These parts provide the signals that give you your sense of balance when you walk, run, dance, or move in other ways.

High pressure in your ears is uncomfortable.

Ear "pops"

Air is light as a feather but it still presses on the body. This pressure is usually the same inside and outside the ear, unless you go up high. Then, pressure in the ears rises and makes the eardrums bulge. The ear "pops" when the eardrum snaps back to its usual position.

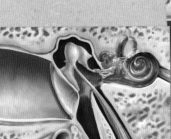

Equal pressure
Pressure inside and outside is equal.

Pressure up
Pressure inside rises; eardrum bulges.

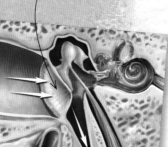

Eardrum

Pressure down
Pressure drops; eardrum pops back.

Semicircular canals

Cochlea

Eustachian tube

Eardrum

Ear canal

Hearing

The flaps we think of as our ears are easy to see but hearing starts in the hidden cochlea. This coiled tube has about 16,000 wispy hair cells that sense sound vibrations and fire nerve impulses to the brain. Sensors for balance link up with the curved semicircular canals.

Hair cells look like threads.

Turn and twist

Bulges in the semicircular canals have sensors that report to your brain on turning or twisting movements. Inside each bulge is a small "cap" called a cupula. When your body turns, the cupula bends and so do hair cells in it. The brain uses the nerve signals they send to order muscle movements that help to keep your balance.

Hair cells

Cupula

Turning
The cupula's hair cells bend when the body turns.

Nerve ending

Up straight
The cupula and hair cells are straight when you stand tall.

Semicircular canals

Vestibular nerve

Utricule

Saccule

Up or down?
When your head moves, fluid in the semicircular canals bends hair cells in sacs called the saccule and utricule, sending nerve signals that "tell" your brain where your head is.

Inner ear

Stirrup (stapes)

Anvil (incus)

Outer ear

Ear canal

Middle ear

Hammer (malleus)

Eardrum

Moving sounds

The outer ear funnels sound waves into the ear canal. The waves push the eardrum against tiny bones in the middle ear. These bones are sometimes called the hammer, anvil, and stirrup. They send sound vibrations on to the inner ear.

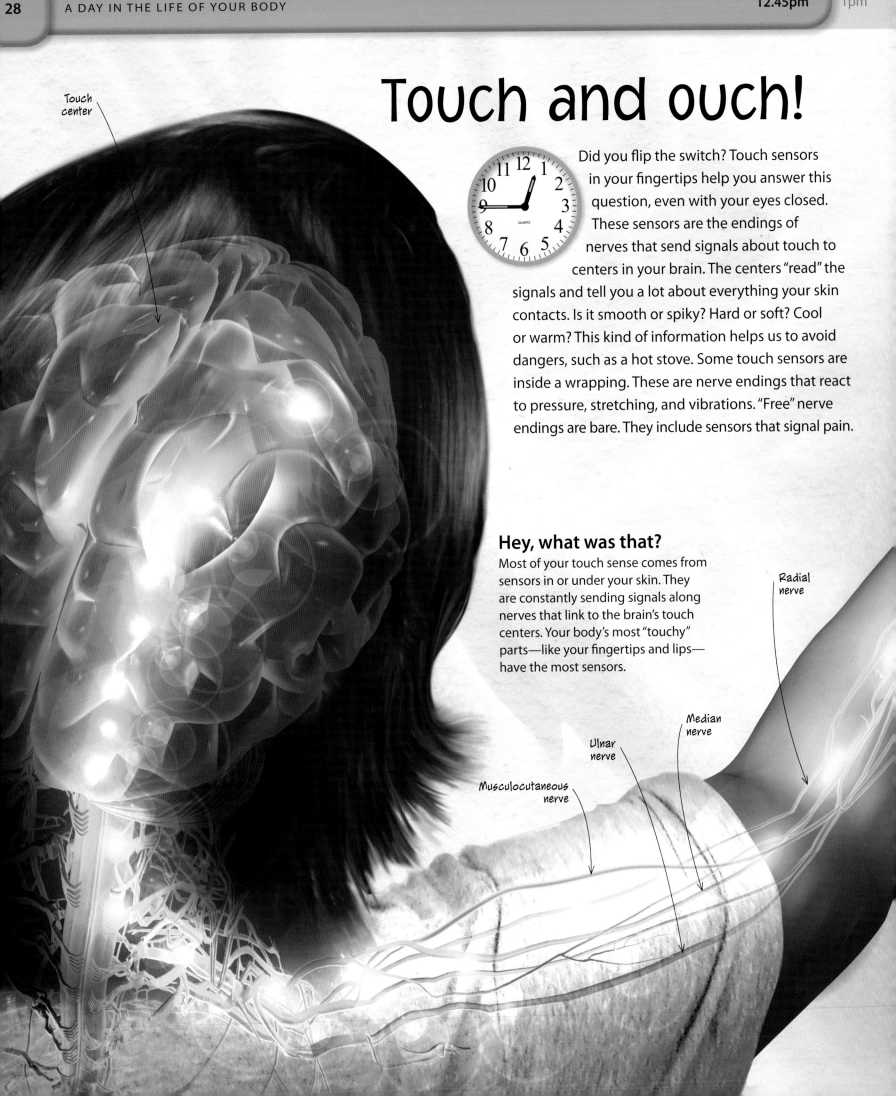

Touch and ouch!

Did you flip the switch? Touch sensors in your fingertips help you answer this question, even with your eyes closed. These sensors are the endings of nerves that send signals about touch to centers in your brain. The centers "read" the signals and tell you a lot about everything your skin contacts. Is it smooth or spiky? Hard or soft? Cool or warm? This kind of information helps us to avoid dangers, such as a hot stove. Some touch sensors are inside a wrapping. These are nerve endings that react to pressure, stretching, and vibrations. "Free" nerve endings are bare. They include sensors that signal pain.

Hey, what was that?

Most of your touch sense comes from sensors in or under your skin. They are constantly sending signals along nerves that link to the brain's touch centers. Your body's most "touchy" parts—like your fingertips and lips—have the most sensors.

Touch center

Radial nerve

Median nerve

Ulnar nerve

Musculocutaneous nerve

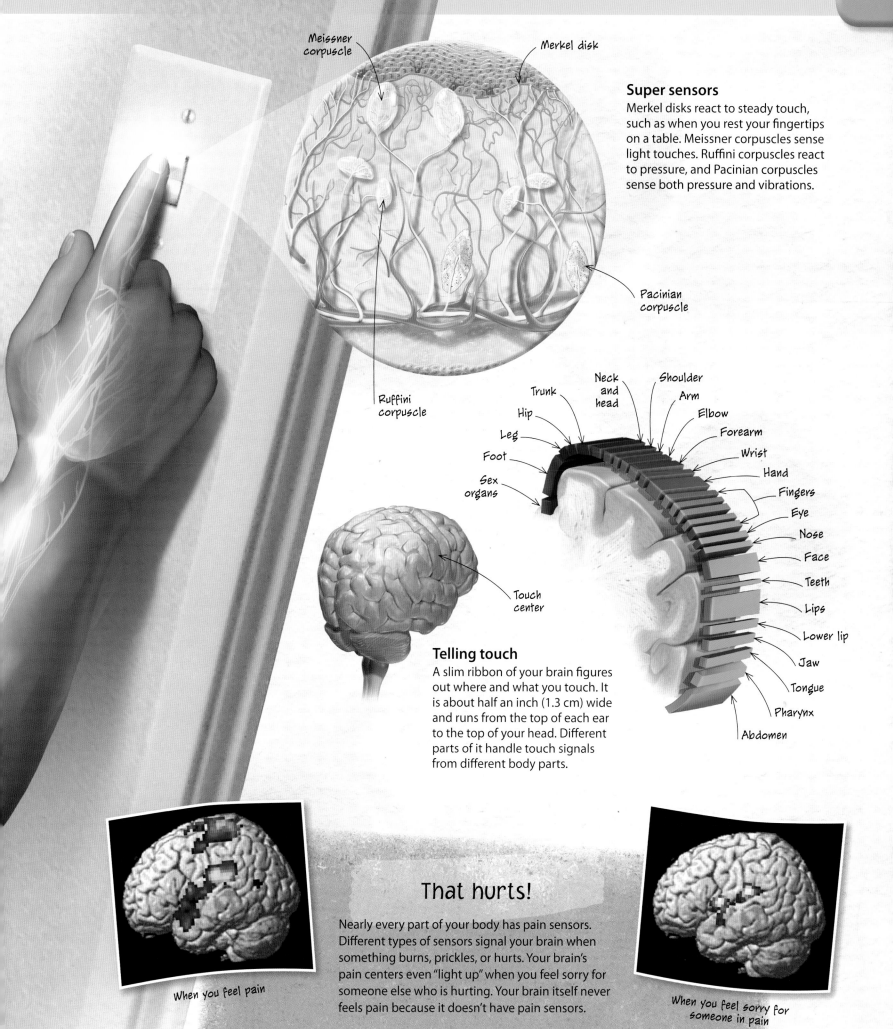

Meissner
corpuscle

Merkel disk

Super sensors

Merkel disks react to steady touch,
such as when you rest your fingertips
on a table. Meissner corpuscles sense
light touches. Ruffini corpuscles react
to pressure, and Pacinian corpuscles
sense both pressure and vibrations.

Pacinian
corpuscle

Ruffini
corpuscle

Neck
and
head

Trunk   Shoulder
Arm
Hip   Elbow
Leg   Forearm
Foot   Wrist
Hand
Sex   Fingers
organs   Eye
Nose
Face
Teeth
Lips
Lower lip
Touch   Jaw
center   Tongue
Pharynx
Abdomen

Telling touch

A slim ribbon of your brain figures
out where and what you touch. It
is about half an inch (1.3 cm) wide
and runs from the top of each ear
to the top of your head. Different
parts of it handle touch signals
from different body parts.

When you feel pain

That hurts!

Nearly every part of your body has pain sensors.
Different types of sensors signal your brain when
something burns, prickles, or hurts. Your brain's
pain centers even "light up" when you feel sorry for
someone else who is hurting. Your brain itself never
feels pain because it doesn't have pain sensors.

When you feel sorry for
someone in pain

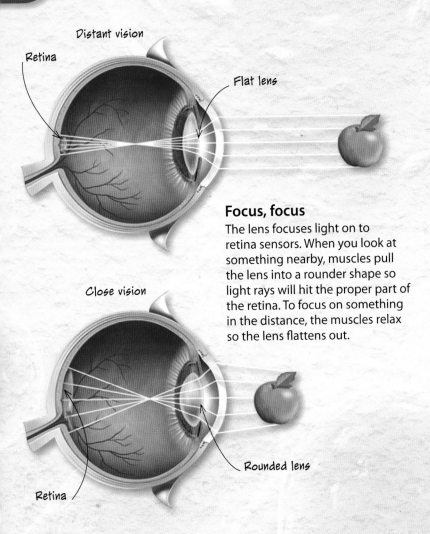

Distant vision

Retina

Flat lens

Focus, focus

The lens focuses light on to retina sensors. When you look at something nearby, muscles pull the lens into a rounder shape so light rays will hit the proper part of the retina. To focus on something in the distance, the muscles relax so the lens flattens out.

Close vision

Rounded lens

Retina

Eyes in action

You use your eyes for reading words and viewing pictures on a screen—in fact, for seeing all the world's sights. An eyeball is only a bit more than 1 inch (2 cm) across, but our seeing sense, or vision, is the most powerful sense of all. We can see hundreds of colors, specks of dust, fuzzy shadows, and all sorts of movements. Eye muscles can move parts inside the eyeball that help you to focus on things that are close by or far away. These feats start with vision sensors in your eyes that react to light. Many more steps in your amazing brain turn the light signals into the scenes and objects you see every day of your life.

Out of focus

Some people have eyeballs that are not the usual ball shape. If the eyeballs are wider than they are tall, the person is nearsighted. This means that the lens can't focus well on faraway objects, so they look blurry. If the eyeballs are taller than they are wide, the person is farsighted. Things in the distance are sharp but close ones are blurred.

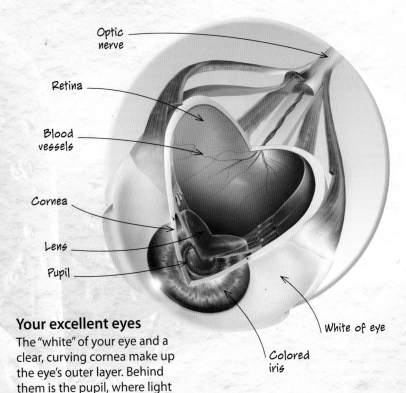

Optic nerve

Retina

Blood vessels

Cornea

Lens

Pupil

White of eye

Colored iris

Your excellent eyes

The "white" of your eye and a clear, curving cornea make up the eye's outer layer. Behind them is the pupil, where light comes into the eye, the colored iris, and a saucer-shaped lens. Light sensors are in the retina.

Signal cross

Light sensors pick up light from an area called an eye's field of vision. A nerve from each eye takes signals from the right side of this field to a vision center in the brain's left half. Signals from the left side of the field go to the brain's right half.

Farsighted
A farsighted person sees the dog like this.

Nearsighted
A nearsighted person sees the dog like this.

Narrow pupil in
bright light

Wide open pupil
in low light

Letting light in

The pupil is the dark "hole" in the middle of the iris. Tiny muscles connected to it control how much light enters an eye. When light is bright, the muscles shrink the opening. In dim light, the pupil opens wider.

Color blindness test

ARE YOU COLOR BLIND?

Some people have trouble telling red from green. This happens when some cones are missing from the retina. This picture is a simple test for red–green color blindness. A person with the usual set of rods and cones can see the number 74 in the middle.

Right
vision
center

Left
vision
center

Nerve
signal

Optic
nerve

Right
eye

Left
eye

Overlapping
vision
fields

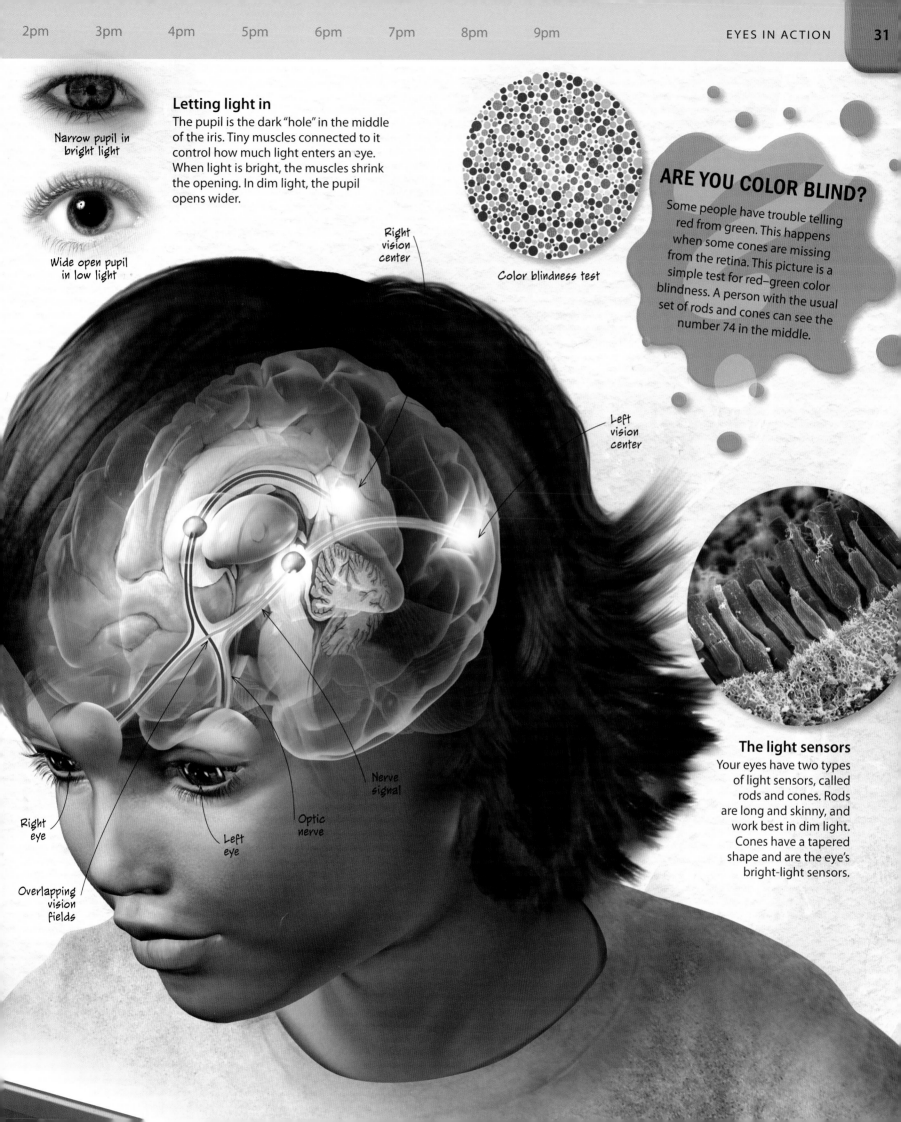

The light sensors

Your eyes have two types of light sensors, called rods and cones. Rods are long and skinny, and work best in dim light. Cones have a tapered shape and are the eye's bright-light sensors.

Empty and full

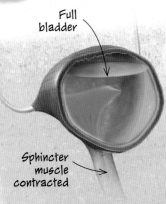

Full bladder

Sphincter muscle contracted

Full bladder
While urine is filling your bladder, you keep the sphincter muscle contracted.

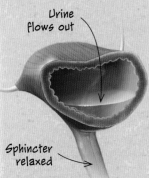

Urine flows out

Sphincter relaxed

Empty bladder
When it's time to "go," you relax the sphincter and urine flows out through your urethra.

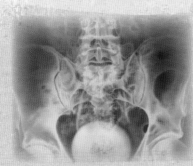

This X-ray photograph shows a bladder expanded, like a strong balloon, as it fills with urine.

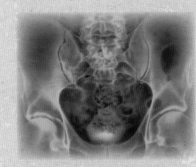

When you go to the bathroom and urinate, the bladder shrinks back to its starting size.

Time to go

Time for a bathroom break? Each day your urinary system handles about 1 quart (1 L) of urine. The urinary system includes your two kidneys and your bladder, plus two ureters and the urethra. Each kidney is about the size of a large, curved dinner roll. Inside each, about 1 million blood filters, called nephrons, form urine from wastes. Ureters are tubes that carry urine to the bladder. As your bladder fills up, its nerve cells signal the brain and you feel the urge to urinate. Young children learn to control the sphincter muscles around the top of the urethra. When it's time to "go," you let the muscles relax so urine can flow down your urethra and out of your body.

Cross section of a kidney
Nephrons are in a kidney's outer part. Substances that they filter from blood flow into a looping tube. Along the way, anything that is useful returns to the blood, but wastes move on into a pipelike duct that opens into the inner kidney.

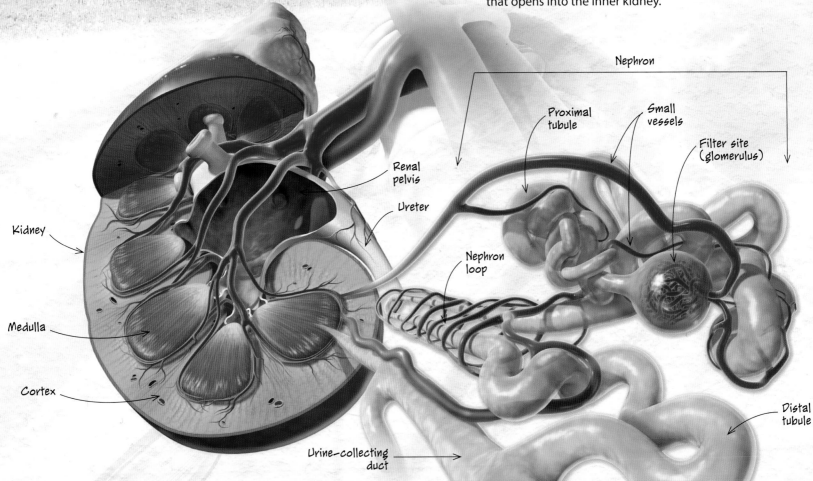

Nephron

Renal pelvis

Ureter

Nephron loop

Kidney

Medulla

Cortex

Urine-collecting duct

Proximal tubule

Small vessels

Filter site (glomerulus)

Distal tubule

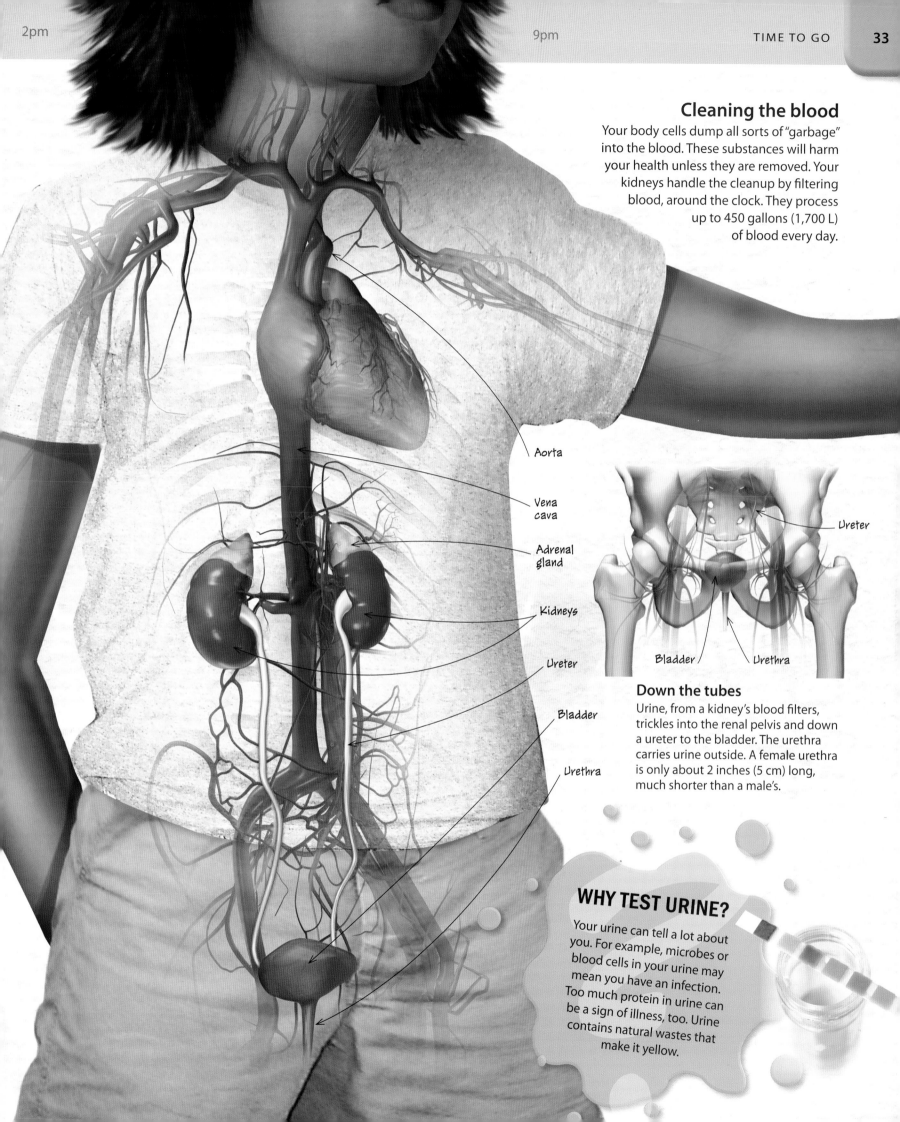

Cleaning the blood

Your body cells dump all sorts of "garbage" into the blood. These substances will harm your health unless they are removed. Your kidneys handle the cleanup by filtering blood, around the clock. They process up to 450 gallons (1,700 L) of blood every day.

Aorta

Vena cava

Adrenal gland

Kidneys

Ureter

Bladder

Urethra

Ureter

Bladder

Urethra

Down the tubes

Urine, from a kidney's blood filters, trickles into the renal pelvis and down a ureter to the bladder. The urethra carries urine outside. A female urethra is only about 2 inches (5 cm) long, much shorter than a male's.

WHY TEST URINE?

Your urine can tell a lot about you. For example, microbes or blood cells in your urine may mean you have an infection. Too much protein in urine can be a sign of illness, too. Urine contains natural wastes that make it yellow.

Healing step by step

Healing begins almost as soon as your skin is damaged. Blood clots plug up torn blood vessels. Helpful substances flood in to help fight microbes. A scab forms as the injured skin repairs itself from the inside out.

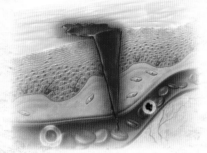

Inflammation
The hurt spot may be red and sore in the first stage of healing.

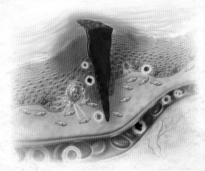

Blood clot
Blood cells and platelets form a clot that plugs torn vessels and stops bleeding.

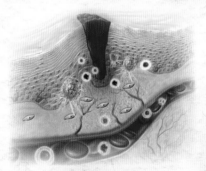

New scab
A scab closes off the injured area while new skin cells form under it.

Scab falls off
When the damage is healed, the scab dries up and falls off.

Clean, check, and go

A lymph node is a filter armed with defender cells. Pockets in the node are where cells, called macrophages, remove and destroy microbes in lymph. Cleansed lymph flows out and into the bloodstream.

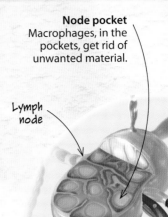

Node pocket
Macrophages, in the pockets, get rid of unwanted material.

Tube out
Once lymph is processed and cleaned, it is returned to the bloodstream.

Lymph node

Macrophage

Tube in
Lymph tubes pick up watery liquid from body tissues and carry it into the node.

Accidents do happen

Ouch! A cut hurts! It may also be a danger to your body. Even small cuts and scratches can let in microbes that may cause an infection. Luckily, the body has strong defenses that are always at hand to help keep you healthy. Unbroken skin stops many intruders in their tracks. Chemicals in your saliva and tears also fight microbes. Most important, you have an immune system that can protect you from many diseases. It works together with the lymphatic system. Your white blood cells are some of the body's main defenders. Some kinds make chemicals called antibodies that help to fight invaders. Others are like scouts that find and kill cells infected by bacteria or a virus.

Sneaky virus

A virus is like a pirate that sneaks into body cells and attacks them. When you have a cold or the flu, a virus is often the culprit. Some kinds of white blood cells can fight viruses by destroying infected cells. The virus, hiding inside, is destroyed, too.

Virus
White blood cells destroy body cells that a virus has infected.

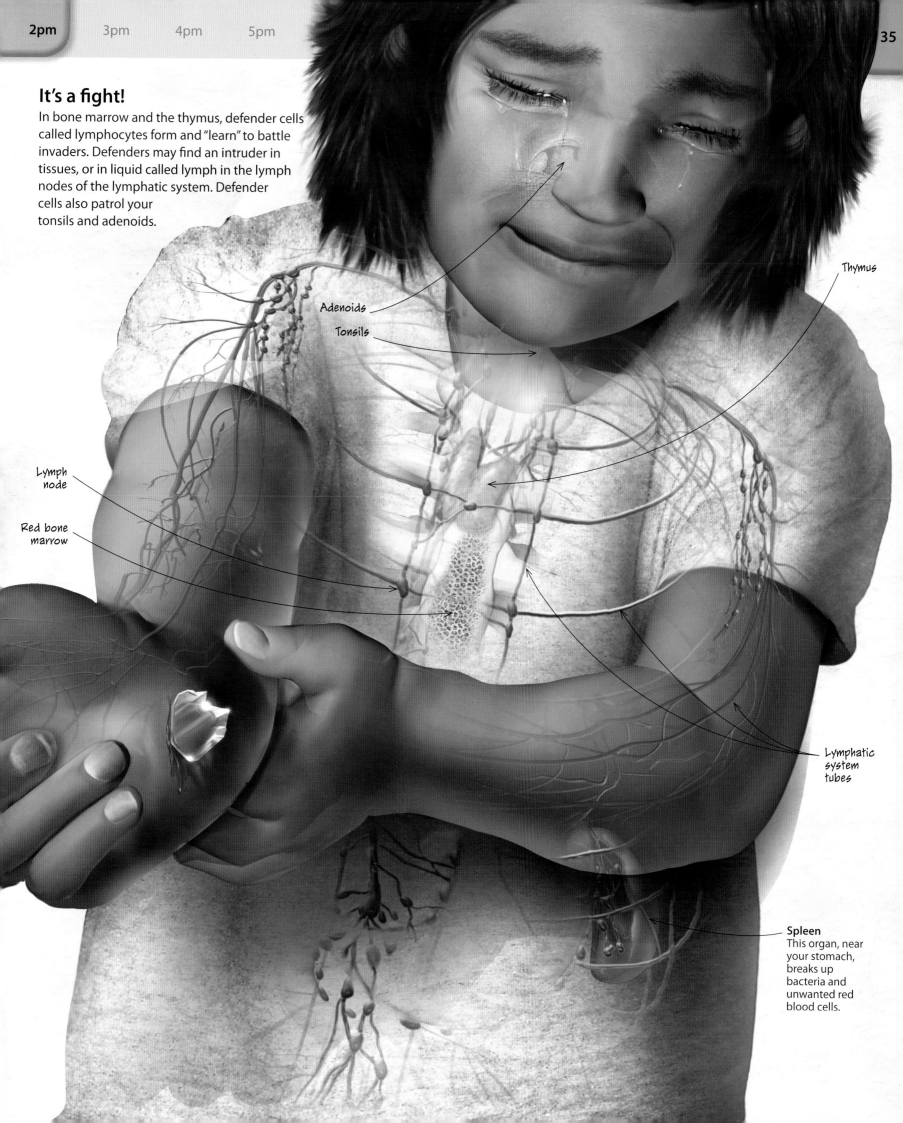

It's a fight!

In bone marrow and the thymus, defender cells called lymphocytes form and "learn" to battle invaders. Defenders may find an intruder in tissues, or in liquid called lymph in the lymph nodes of the lymphatic system. Defender cells also patrol your tonsils and adenoids.

Thymus

Adenoids

Tonsils

Lymph node

Red bone marrow

Lymphatic system tubes

Spleen
This organ, near your stomach, breaks up bacteria and unwanted red blood cells.

Doctor, doctor

For a deep cut or nasty gash, a visit to the doctor is a good way to make sure that you don't get a dangerous infection. Dirt that gets into a cut may have harmful bacteria in it. Some of these microbes can make you very sick. The doctor will start by cleaning the cut and wiping on an antiseptic that helps to kill harmful germs. If there is a big hole or tear in your skin, stitches may be used to close it up. Your doctor may also give you an injection or "shot" of medicine that works inside your body to help prevent the disease tetanus. A bandage helps to protect the wound and keep it clean while it heals.

Tetanus danger

Harmful bacteria in a wound can cause the disease tetanus. The microbes make a poison that stops muscles from working properly. You couldn't breathe if muscles in your chest were affected.

Poison!
Tetanus bacteria make a toxin that poisons nerves controlling your muscles.

Getting a tetanus "booster"

When you were younger, you probably got a shot to prevent tetanus. The shot turns on defender cells in your lymph nodes. These cells make antibodies that attack the tetanus toxin.

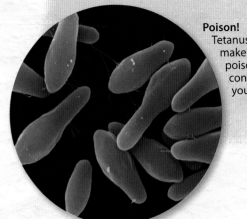

More antibodies, please
You need plenty of antibodies to fight tetanus. It can take a few days for defender cells in your lymph nodes to make these antibodies. To be on the safe side, your doctor may give you a shot of antibodies that go to work right away.

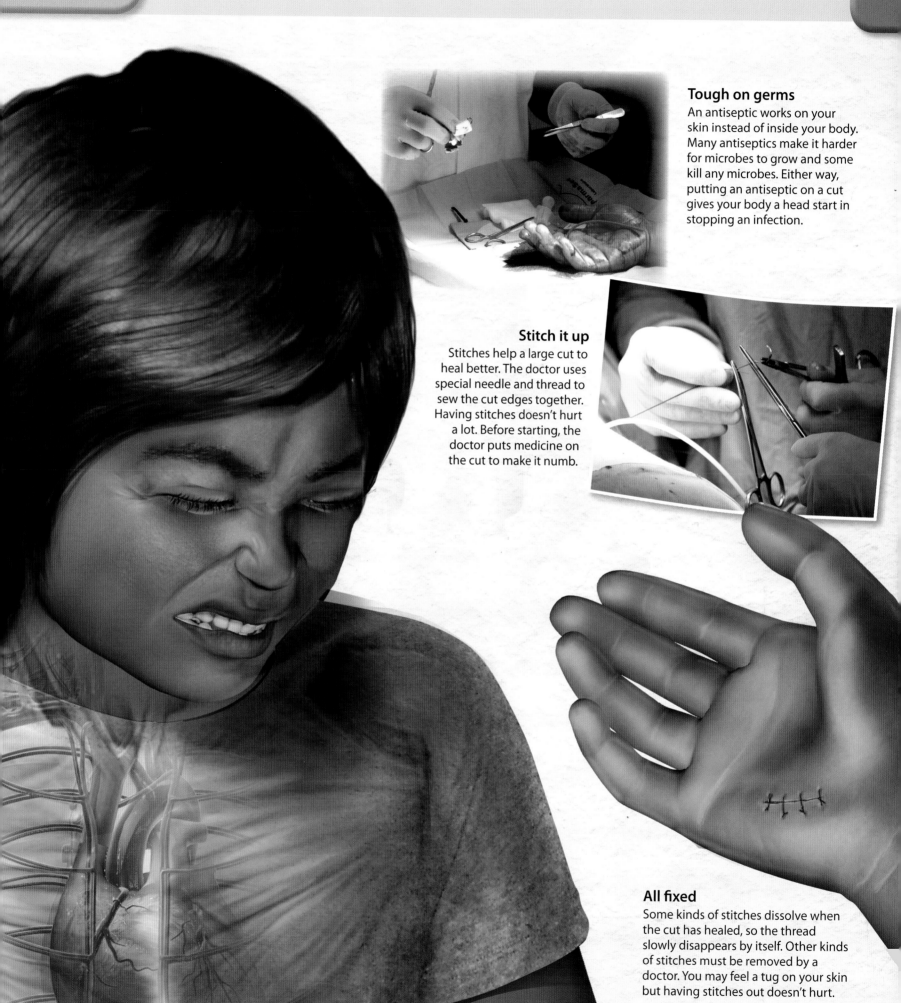

Tough on germs

An antiseptic works on your skin instead of inside your body. Many antiseptics make it harder for microbes to grow and some kill any microbes. Either way, putting an antiseptic on a cut gives your body a head start in stopping an infection.

Stitch it up

Stitches help a large cut to heal better. The doctor uses special needle and thread to sew the cut edges together. Having stitches doesn't hurt a lot. Before starting, the doctor puts medicine on the cut to make it numb.

All fixed

Some kinds of stitches dissolve when the cut has healed, so the thread slowly disappears by itself. Other kinds of stitches must be removed by a doctor. You may feel a tug on your skin but having stitches out doesn't hurt.

All in the family

How did you get the shape of your nose or the color of your eyes? You inherited genes from your parents. Genes give the "orders" for building and running your body from head to toe. You have about 19,500 different genes, and all of them are made from a chemical called DNA. DNA is amazing—it can give instructions for making all the different parts of your body and for all the jobs they must do. Your genes aren't all lumped together, however. They are divided into groups, a bit like separate strings of beads. Each group of genes is called a chromosome. There are 23 kinds of chromosomes. Like shoes, you have pairs of them—one from your mother and one from your father.

Child's chromosomes

1 1
2 2
3 3
4 4
5 5
6 6
7 7
8 8
9 9
10 10
11 11
12 12
13 13
14 14
15 15
16 16
17 17
18 18
19 19
20 20
21 21
22 22
X Y

Some of mother's DNA
You have genes that were on the chromosomes your mother passed on to you.

Child's DNA
Each pair of your chromosomes includes one from Mom and one from Dad.

Some of father's DNA
You also have genes that were on the chromosomes you received from your father.

Girl or boy?

One chromosome pair has genes that determine whether a baby is a girl or a boy. The chromosomes in this pair are called sex chromosomes. The sex chromosome you inherited from your mother was an X chromosome. From your father you inherited either an X or a Y. You are a girl if you received an XX pair. If you got an XY pair, you are a boy.

XX

XY

X and Y chromosomes
An X sex chromosome is much larger and has more genes than a Y sex chromosome.

Sperm contains 23 chromosomes

Sperm meets egg
A male sperm and a female egg each have 23 single chromosomes. When they unite, there are 23 pairs.

Egg contains 23 chromosomes

Mother's chromosomes

1 1
2 2
3 3
4 4
5 5
6 6
7 7
8 8
9 9
10 10
11 11
12 12
13 13
14 14
15 15
16 16
17 17
18 18
19 19
20 20
21 21
22 22
X X

Father's chromosomes

1 1
2 2
3 3
4 4
5 5
6 6
7 7
8 8
9 9
10 10
11 11
12 12
13 13
14 14
15 15
16 16
17 17
18 18
19 19
20 20
21 21
22 22
X Y

Chromosome close-up
The two chromosomes of each pair link up in the middle.

Who do you look like?

Unless you have an identical twin, no one else looks exactly like you. The chromosomes you inherited formed with your personal set of genes. If you have siblings (sisters or brothers), they also inherited chromosomes from each of your parents. But their "personal" genes are not all the same as yours.

Siblings do not look alike

Siblings look alike

Family genes
You received one of the chromosomes in each pair that your mother and father have. Information from the genes on these chromosomes determined your nose shape, your skin color, your sex, and more.

DNA's shape
DNA is built something like a ladder that is twisted into a spiral. This shape is called a double helix. Each gene is a section of the ladder. In a chromosome, the helix coils up, which helps to keep the DNA from getting tangled.

Processing food

Is dinner ready? Good! Your body uses nutrients in food for fuel and to make new cells and tissues as you grow. The processes that make energy and build body tissues are called metabolism. Carbohydrates, proteins, and fats top the list of basic food nutrients. Nutritious food also has vitamins and minerals, which are used in your nervous system, muscles, bones, and other parts.

Carbohydrates are the body's most important source of energy. They provide the sugar glucose, which we sometimes call "blood sugar" because the blood carries it all through your body. This substance is the main fuel for all your cells. When you eat a healthy diet and get lots of exercise, you help to keep your body in tip-top shape.

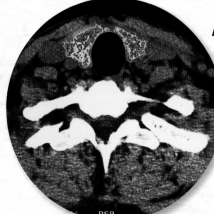

An energy controller
The orange "butterfly" in this scan is the thyroid gland in the neck. It makes a hormone that controls how your cells use energy. You also need a proper amount of this hormone to grow normally.

Thyroid close-up
Every day, your thyroid helps to keep your energy level and your body temperature normal. If a person feels tired a lot of the time, the doctor may check to see if the thyroid is working as it should.

Eat enough, no more

Calories are how we measure the energy in food. Your meals and snacks should provide enough calories to keep your brain, muscles, and other parts working well. The basic amount of energy you use in a day is called your basal metabolic rate, or BMR. If you often eat more calories than your body needs, the extra may turn to unhealthy body fat.

Salad
A green salad has carbohydrates and lots of vitamins.

Potatoes
Potatoes have carbohydrates and important minerals.

Meat
Meat, fish, beans, and dairy foods are protein champions.

Healthy weight

Overweight

What's on your plate?
A healthy meal will have complex carbohydrates, like salad or vegetables, some protein, and a bit of fat. Food also contains substances that your cells use to make DNA.

Let's eat!

Do you look forward to eating dinner? That's your appetite at work! Hormones from your digestive system signal your brain in ways that affect your appetite. If you are upset, you might not feel like eating. If you're having a favorite food for dinner, you may keep eating even after you are full.

Leptin
This hormone from body fat reduces appetite.

PYY
PYY from the small intestine reduces your appetite after a meal.

Insulin
After you eat, insulin from the pancreas reduces your appetite.

Grehlin
This stomach hormone increases appetite.

Thyroid gland

Liver

Stomach

Pancreas

Blood sugar
Your cells get sugar from the bloodstream for energy. Hormones from your pancreas control this process. Your liver will store some leftover sugar. The rest may be turned into body fat.

Dinner time
At dinner you enjoy a tasty meal and stock up on energy for the night ahead. Your pancreas and liver work together to ensure a steady supply of glucose in your bloodstream. Your cells will have enough fuel even though you may not eat again for many hours.

Grow tall, grow up

Time to measure up! From the time you were born until you are a young adult, your body will be getting a bit larger and taller almost every day. When you were very young, you probably had some growth "spurts" when you grew taller very fast. You will have another big growth spurt when you reach puberty. This is the time when your reproductive organs grow to adult size and start to make sex hormones. Puberty brings lots of changes to the body, including underarm hair and pubic hair. By the time puberty ends, your body will be well on its way to the size and shape it will be when you are an adult. If you are male, your voice will change and you will grow facial hair. If you are female, you will start to develop breasts and a curvier body.

Changing times

The proportions of your body parts change while you are growing up. Your brain and head grew large quickly, while you were a baby and toddler. From the age of five to the age of 10, a child's legs get much longer compared to other parts of the body.

Growth hormone

The pituitary gland in the brain makes growth hormone, or GH. This hormone makes your muscles grow bigger. When it acts on cells in the liver, they make a substance that causes bones to grow longer. GH also helps the body to burn fat.

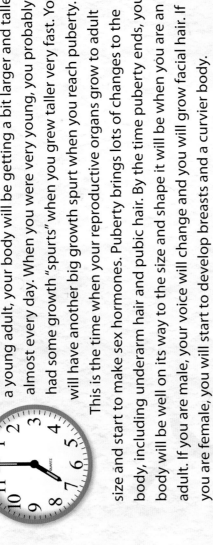

Estimated height at 15 years

Height at 10 years

Hypothalamus

Pituitary gland

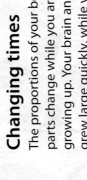

Height at 5 years

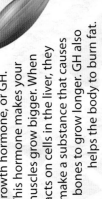

Liver

Pituitary gland

Bones

Fat

Skeletal muscles

Female reproductive system

A female's reproductive system includes two ovaries and the uterus. Ovaries make eggs that can unite with a male's sperm. This is the first step in a pregnancy. A baby grows in the uterus. It passes through the woman's vagina when it is born.

Breasts
Breasts have glands that can produce milk.

Uterus
This is where a baby develops before birth.

Adult female
The hormone estrogen gives a female adult breasts and a curvy body shape. She also has a menstrual cycle. Each month, the lining of the uterus is made ready for a baby to develop. If there is no pregnancy, the lining is expelled.

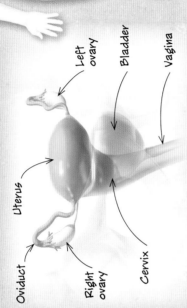

Left ovary

Bladder

Vagina

Uterus

Oviduct

Right ovary

Cervix

Male reproductive system

A male's reproductive system includes his penis, testicles, and some glands and tubes. Testicles or testes are where sperm form. A tube called the epididymis connects to each testicle and stores sperm. The prostate gland and seminal vesicles make a liquid called semen that carries sperm to the outside.

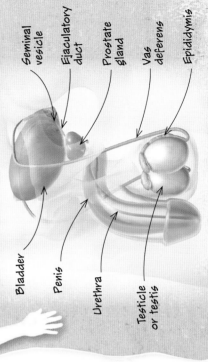

Seminal vesicle

Ejaculatory duct

Prostate gland

Vas deferens

Epididymis

Bladder

Penis

Urethra

Testicle or testis

Testosterone
The male hormone testosterone is produced inside the testicles.

Adult male
The hormone testosterone shapes the body of an adult male. He has larger, stronger muscles and a deeper voice than a boy. He also has much more body hair, including whiskers on his face.

What is sleep?

Sleep has long been a mystery. To study what goes on in the brain during sleep, scientists use sensors called electrodes that attach to the head of a sleeping person. They pick up signals from brain cells and send them to a machine called an electroencephalograph. By studying how these signals change during sleep, a scientist can see which parts of the brain are busy at different times.

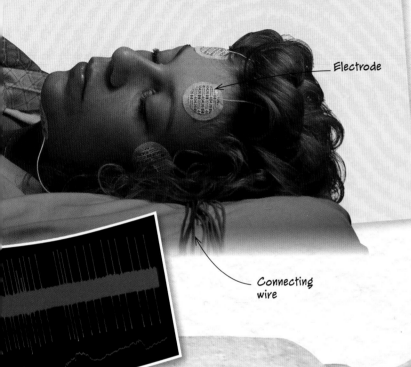

Electrode

Connecting wire

Sleep activity
Here, a sleeper's eye movements show up pink on a computer screen. The blue line below shows brain activity.

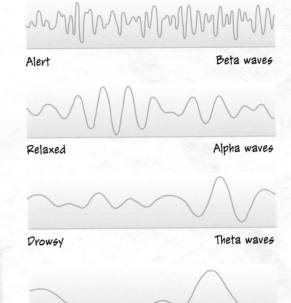

Alert   Beta waves

Relaxed   Alpha waves

Drowsy   Theta waves

Sleeping   Delta waves

Brain waves

Brain waves show nerve cells at work in the thinking areas of your brain. Beta waves form when you are alert. Alpha waves form when you are relaxed. When you feel drowsy, your brain makes theta waves. Delta waves indicate you are asleep.

Heart
Your heart beats a little more slowly when you sleep.

Lung
You don't breathe as deeply when you sleep.

Rest and sleep

Nearly all parts of your body take much-needed rest when you sleep. Your circulatory system, respiratory system, and muscles all do less work. People who don't get enough sleep can't think as clearly. Doing well in any activity is much harder if you are tired.

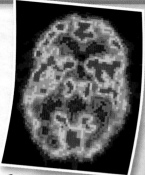

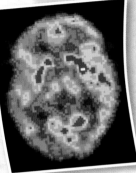

Dreaming (REM) sleep

Non-REM sleep

Dreaming

Dreams are one of the puzzles of sleep. People young and old dream. Even small babies do. Some people dream every night. Others may never dream. You may or may not remember your dreams. Tests show that parts of the brain are very active during a dream. Some scientists think that dreams help the brain to organize the many things you feel, think, or worry about while you are awake.

The clock winds down

What a day! Now your body needs rest. Sleep also gives your brain a chance to shift gears. Brain centers that manage your breathing and other basic tasks stay busy, but the brain's "thinking" parts slow down. By studying sleeping people, scientists have learned that the brain switches between two different kinds of sleep. REM, or Rapid Eye Movement, sleep is the stage when you are likely to dream. Your eyes move rapidly under your eyelids while you are "seeing" a dream. NREM (meaning non-REM) stages are when you sleep without dreaming much. Both kinds of sleep are important for the brain to operate at its best during the coming day.

Brain stem
Nerve cells here keep basic body functions going during sleep.

Hearing
Your hearing works while you sleep, so sounds can wake you.

Pineal gland
This gland tracks the shift from daytime to night.

Hypothalamus
The hypothalamus is the main sleep controller.

Pituitary
This gland boosts the supply of some hormones before you wake.

Muscles
Many muscles can't contract while you are sleeping deeply.

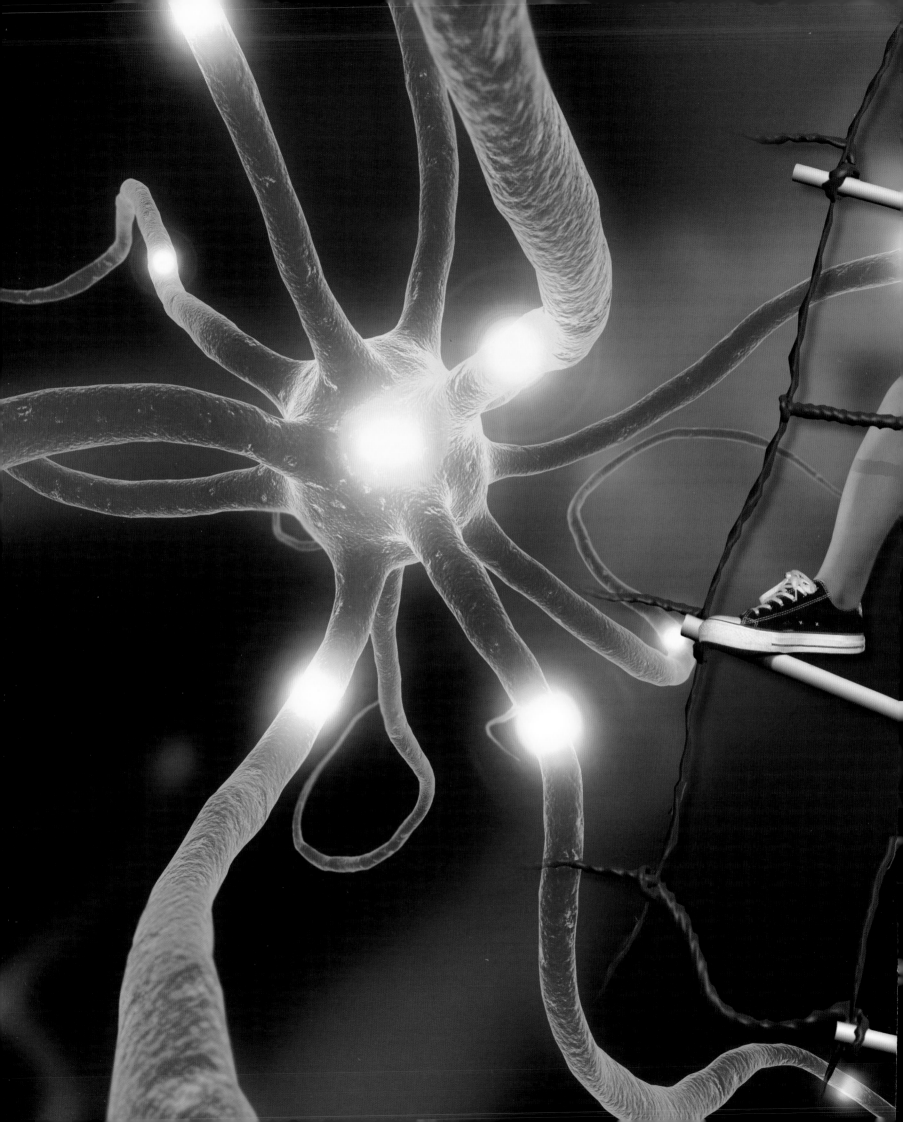

Long
LIFE

Cells

Cells are the building blocks of all living things. A cell is the smallest bit of life we know—so small that most cells can only be seen with a microscope. Your body has about 200 different kinds of cells. All have the same basic parts, but each kind of cell also has its own special task in the body. The different types of cells must work together to keep the whole body functioning properly. For example, it takes at least two different kinds of cells to make up a body tissue, like muscle, skin, bone, or brain tissue.

Connective tissue
This connective tissue has fibers and other material that help the tissue to perform its function.

Types of tissue

The body has four kinds of tissue. Muscle cells are the main ingredients in muscle tissue. Nervous tissue is mainly nerve cells. Your skin is an epithelial tissue. Connective tissue connects and supports body parts.

Epithelial tissue
In the epithelial tissue lining airways to your lungs, tiny hairs help to trap dirt and microbes.

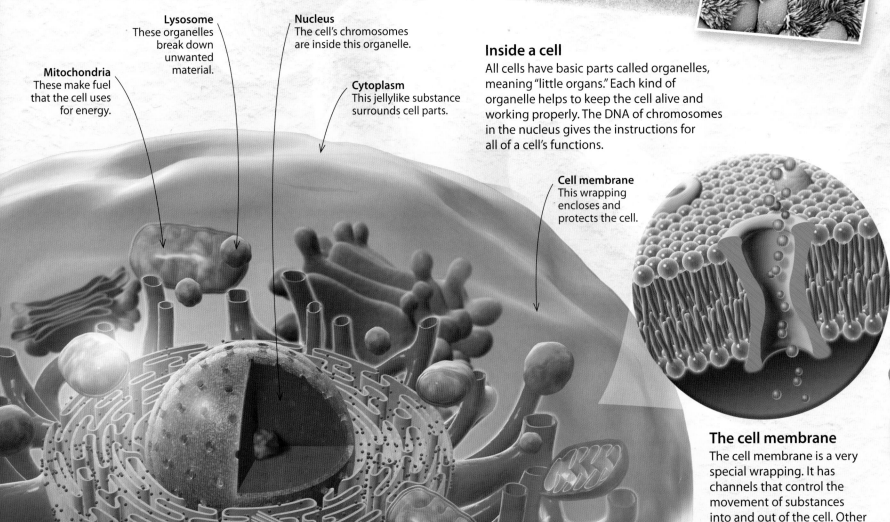

Lysosome
These organelles break down unwanted material.

Nucleus
The cell's chromosomes are inside this organelle.

Mitochondria
These make fuel that the cell uses for energy.

Cytoplasm
This jellylike substance surrounds cell parts.

Inside a cell

All cells have basic parts called organelles, meaning "little organs." Each kind of organelle helps to keep the cell alive and working properly. The DNA of chromosomes in the nucleus gives the instructions for all of a cell's functions.

Cell membrane
This wrapping encloses and protects the cell.

The cell membrane

The cell membrane is a very special wrapping. It has channels that control the movement of substances into and out of the cell. Other parts of the membrane help the cell to receive signals.

Nerve cell
The thin extensions
of this motor neuron
carry signals to cells in
muscles and glands.

Cells and cell shapes

Each kind of body cell has a
shape that suits its job. Long,
skinny muscle cells allow
movement. Nerve cells have
extensions that pick up or send
signals. The round, bag-like
shape of adipose cells allows
them to store fat.

Red blood cells
Red blood cells
are thin disks.
This shape makes
it easy to pick up and
deliver oxygen.

Epithelial cell
These cells help form skin
and the linings of body
cavities and organs. Many
have a boxy shape.

HOW DO CELLS DIVIDE?

Body cells can divide in two.
The cell makes an extra set
of chromosomes and DNA
instructions. When it divides, each
new cell gets its own set. This
splitting is called mitosis.
It makes new cells as you grow
or to heal a wound.

**Skeletal
muscle cell**
In this muscle cell,
the nucleus is colored brown
and its energy factories
(mitochondria) look yellow.

Adipose cell
An adipose cell is like
a tiny balloon that
can fill up with fat.

Cycling
Your body uses about 60 calories (250 kJ) when you ride a bike for 15 minutes.

Swimming
Swim for 15 minutes and your body will use about 75 calories (315 kJ).

Staying fit and healthy

How can you make sure that every day is a good one for your body? Eating well is a great start. Nutritious foods give you vitamins, minerals, and other raw materials your cells need to work properly. The body also uses water in many ways. Drinking plenty of healthy liquids ensures that your cells and tissues will have the water they need. Being active in the playground and at home will help keep your muscles, bones, and other parts strong and healthy. A good night's sleep will keep your brain sharp and let your growing body rest for the good day to come.

Running
Running uses about 60 calories (250 kJ) every 15 minutes— but it depends on how fast you go.

Walking
Fifteen minutes of walking will use about 40 calories (170 kJ) of energy.

Sitting
For every 15 minutes you spend sitting, your body "burns" only about 8 calories (35 kJ).

Climbing stairs
You use about 70 calories (295 kJ) if you climb stairs for 15 minutes—that's a lot of stairs!

Good sleep

Sleeping is one of the most important things you do. Too little sleep changes the way your brain works. It will be harder to think about schoolwork and you may feel cranky, too. Being tired can also make you clumsy, so you are more likely to stumble or drop things. If you are under the age of 16, you need at least 8–10 hours of sleep most nights.

Feeling tired
Feeling tired and sleepy during the day is a sign that you may need more sleep at night.

Use that energy!
Calories (or kilojoules) are the way we measure energy in food. Most people eat more calories than their bodies need. Using the extra energy to run, swim, or be active in other ways helps to prevent unhealthy body fat from forming.

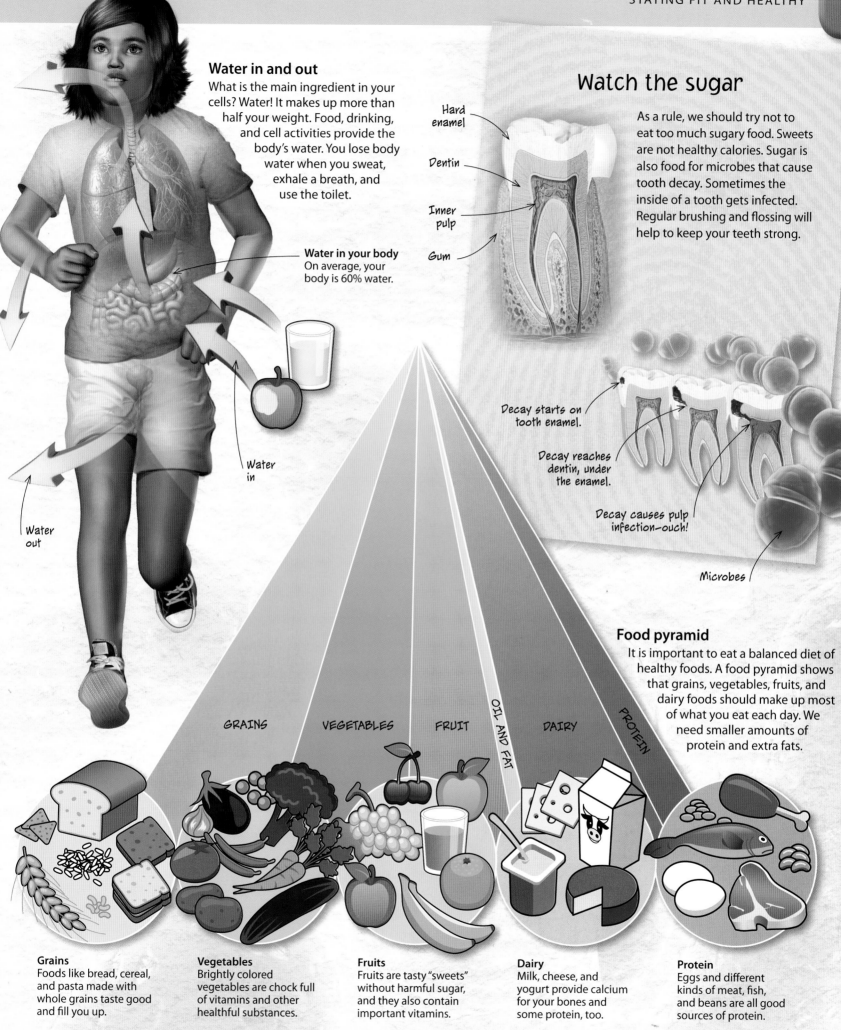

Water in and out

What is the main ingredient in your cells? Water! It makes up more than half your weight. Food, drinking, and cell activities provide the body's water. You lose body water when you sweat, exhale a breath, and use the toilet.

Water in your body
On average, your body is 60% water.

Water in

Water out

Watch the sugar

Hard enamel

Dentin

Inner pulp

Gum

As a rule, we should try not to eat too much sugary food. Sweets are not healthy calories. Sugar is also food for microbes that cause tooth decay. Sometimes the inside of a tooth gets infected. Regular brushing and flossing will help to keep your teeth strong.

Decay starts on tooth enamel.

Decay reaches dentin, under the enamel.

Decay causes pulp infection—ouch!

Microbes

Food pyramid

It is important to eat a balanced diet of healthy foods. A food pyramid shows that grains, vegetables, fruits, and dairy foods should make up most of what you eat each day. We need smaller amounts of protein and extra fats.

GRAINS   VEGETABLES   FRUIT   OIL AND FAT   DAIRY   PROTEIN

Grains
Foods like bread, cereal, and pasta made with whole grains taste good and fill you up.

Vegetables
Brightly colored vegetables are chock full of vitamins and other healthful substances.

Fruits
Fruits are tasty "sweets" without harmful sugar, and they also contain important vitamins.

Dairy
Milk, cheese, and yogurt provide calcium for your bones and some protein, too.

Protein
Eggs and different kinds of meat, fish, and beans are all good sources of protein.

Health: myths and facts

? Do you want to be healthy? You bet! It's also natural to wonder if you are doing something that might harm your body or make some part of it work less well. The truth is, we hear about lots of "health rules," but only some of them are good advice. Experts who study how the body works say that some common health "facts" are really myths.

Myth: You must drink at least eight glasses of water a day.

Fact: How much water does your body need? It depends partly on how active you are. If you exercise a lot or spend time outdoors when it's warm, you may need more than at other times. Drink water when you are thirsty and you should be fine.

Myth: Eating carrots makes you see better in the dark.

Fact: Carrots contain vitamin A but so do some other vegetables, fruits, milk, and eggs. Your eyes need a small amount of vitamin A for normal vision in all kinds of light. If you already eat a balanced diet, eating carrots won't make any difference to how well you see at night.

Myth: Reading in bad light harms your eyes.

Fact: Reading in dim light doesn't harm your eyes although it can cause temporary eyestrain. Then your eyes feel uncomfortable because their muscles get overtired. Watching TV or looking at a computer screen for a long time can also cause eyestrain.

Myth: Eating chocolate and fried food causes acne pimples.

Fact: Clogged pores, overactive oil glands, and some bacteria cause acne. No foods, even fatty ones like chocolate or French fries, make pimples worse. Changes in your hormones, especially at puberty, often cause pimples because they make oil glands more active.

Myth: You will get cramps if you swim less than an hour after eating.

Fact: After you eat, more blood than usual flows to your digestive system. If you use your muscles to swim soon after you've eaten a large or fatty meal, you might get cramps because blood will be diverted away from your stomach and intestines. You can swim sooner if you eat a light meal.

Myth: Your heart stops beating whenever you sneeze.

Fact: Your heart beats normally when you sneeze. The idea that it might stop, or that a sneeze might let evil spirits into the body, are old myths. This may be why people long ago said "Bless you!" after a sneeze, to protect the sneezer against harm.

Myth: Eating sugar makes children overactive.

Fact: Experts who study children say that they cannot find any evidence that sugary food affects how children behave. However, parents often say that they see changes in how a child acts after eating sweets. No one knows for sure, and many scientists are trying to learn more about this question.

Myth: Most of your body heat escapes from your head.

Fact: The body loses heat through any area of exposed skin, whether it is on your head or some other place. If you wear a hat or headscarf, you'll lose less heat from your head. If you cover up but leave your head bare, more of your body heat will be lost there.

Bugs and other bothers

People get sick for many reasons, but "bugs" are high on the list. Bacteria and viruses, organisms called fungi, and parasites can all infect the body. These attackers are called pathogens, which means that they cause harm. Bacteria are tiny cells and not all are harmful, but those that are cause many kinds of infections. Viruses cause most colds and all kinds of influenza—the "flu." Fungi cause many skin diseases and some other ills. Parasites, like lice, are the largest pathogens—so big it is often fairly easy to see them.

Attack by fungi

Believe it or not, harmful fungi are relatives of mushrooms. They cause problems like ringworm. This skin disease got its name because it grows in a ring shape. Another fungus causes athlete's foot between the toes.

Tiny viruses

A virus is a tiny particle that can only survive inside a cell. It's easy to inhale a flu or cold virus after an ill person sneezes or coughs. Contaminated food or water may carry viruses that cause stomach flu and diarrhea.

Protection

A vaccination is a "shot" that helps your immune system to fight pathogens. Babies and young children are often vaccinated against some common viruses, like the one that causes measles. Your parents may also want you to get a flu shot.

Allergies

With an allergy, the immune system "attacks" something that isn't usually harmful. Lots of people get the itchy eyes and stuffy nose of "hay fever" caused by plant pollen. Peanuts, shellfish, and eggs are common causes of food allergies that produce red, itchy skin patches called hives.

Antibiotics

Antibiotics are medicines that kill bacteria and some other kinds of pathogens. Most antibiotics are taken as pills or liquids.

Help on the way
If an allergy causes breathing problems, a person can inject quick-acting medicine from a special "pen."

Hives caused by allergic reaction

Really bad bugs

It's a mistake to stop taking medicine early. When people misuse antibiotics, some bacteria become resistant. This means that the antibiotic can no longer kill the bacteria.

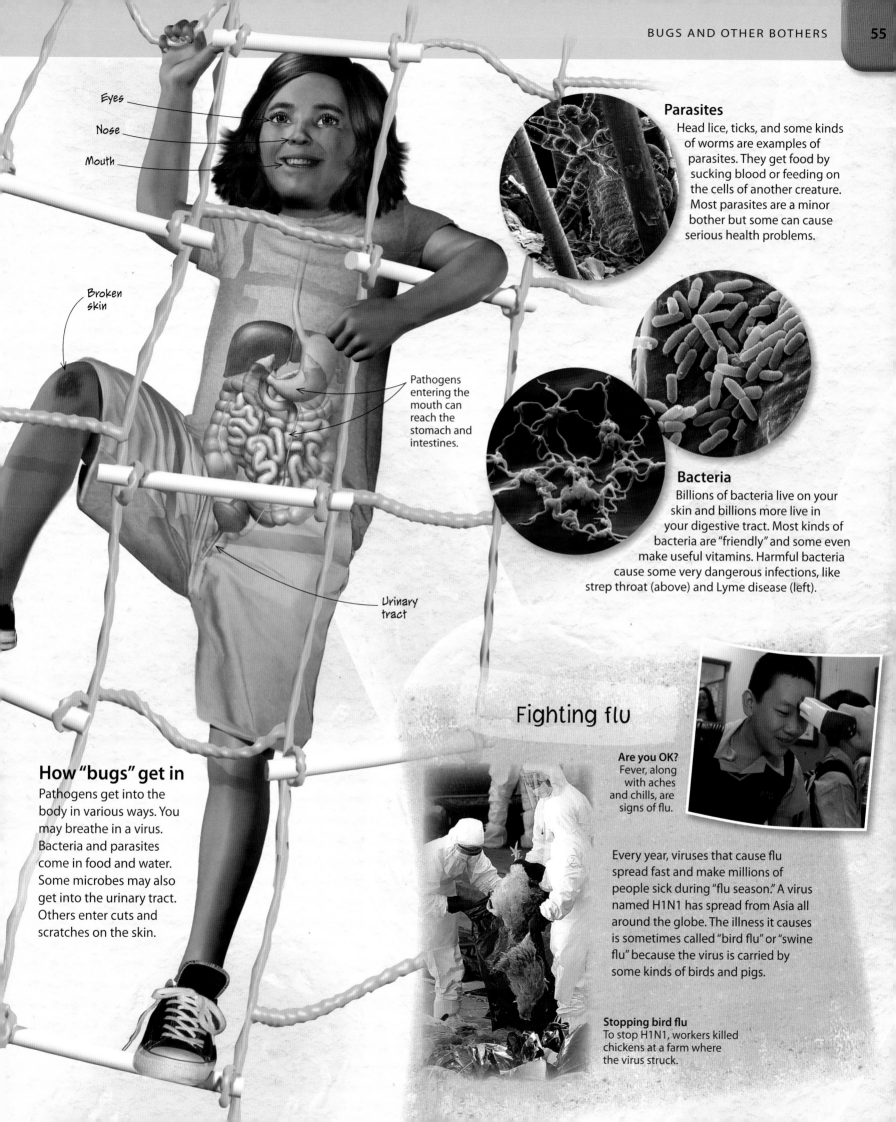

Eyes

Nose

Mouth

Broken skin

Pathogens entering the mouth can reach the stomach and intestines.

Urinary tract

Parasites

Head lice, ticks, and some kinds of worms are examples of parasites. They get food by sucking blood or feeding on the cells of another creature. Most parasites are a minor bother but some can cause serious health problems.

Bacteria

Billions of bacteria live on your skin and billions more live in your digestive tract. Most kinds of bacteria are "friendly" and some even make useful vitamins. Harmful bacteria cause some very dangerous infections, like strep throat (above) and Lyme disease (left).

How "bugs" get in

Pathogens get into the body in various ways. You may breathe in a virus. Bacteria and parasites come in food and water. Some microbes may also get into the urinary tract. Others enter cuts and scratches on the skin.

Fighting flu

Are you OK?
Fever, along with aches and chills, are signs of flu.

Every year, viruses that cause flu spread fast and make millions of people sick during "flu season." A virus named H1N1 has spread from Asia all around the globe. The illness it causes is sometimes called "bird flu" or "swine flu" because the virus is carried by some kinds of birds and pigs.

Stopping bird flu
To stop H1N1, workers killed chickens at a farm where the virus struck.

Children around the world

Are you one of the world's lucky children? If so, you have enough to eat, clean water to drink, and you can visit a doctor when you get sick. For some children and their families, these basics are hard to come by. In poor countries, food, and especially proteins the body needs, may be lacking. Water may contain parasites and bacteria that cause diseases. Often there are very few doctors and nurses. In rich countries, kids have challenges, too. More and more children are developing health problems related to eating unhealthy food and getting too little exercise.

Long life, short life

In rich countries, babies born today will get vaccinations and other health care that prevent many serious diseases. On average, they will live at least 75 years. In poor countries, today's babies may live only to about 45–50 years.

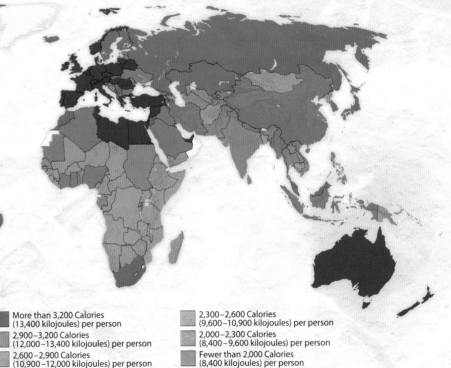

Food differences

If a child doesn't have much food, the body will get only small amounts of important nutrients and food energy, or calories (kilojoules). In poor countries, the average child gets far fewer calories than a child who is lucky enough to live elsewhere.

■ More than 3,200 Calories (13,400 kilojoules) per person	■ 2,300–2,600 Calories (9,600–10,900 kilojoules) per person
■ 2,900–3,200 Calories (12,000–13,400 kilojoules) per person	■ 2,000–2,300 Calories (8,400–9,600 kilojoules) per person
■ 2,600–2,900 Calories (10,900–12,000 kilojoules) per person	■ Fewer than 2,000 Calories (8,400 kilojoules) per person
	□ Not known

Too little food

It is a sad fact that millions of children in poor countries get so little nourishing food that their growth is stunted. They may also have serious health problems due to a lack of vitamins and minerals.

Too much food

Eating too much food can lead to obesity, which is an unhealthy excess of body fat. More and more children in wealthy nations are becoming obese. As a result, more children than ever before have health problems that stem from being so overweight.

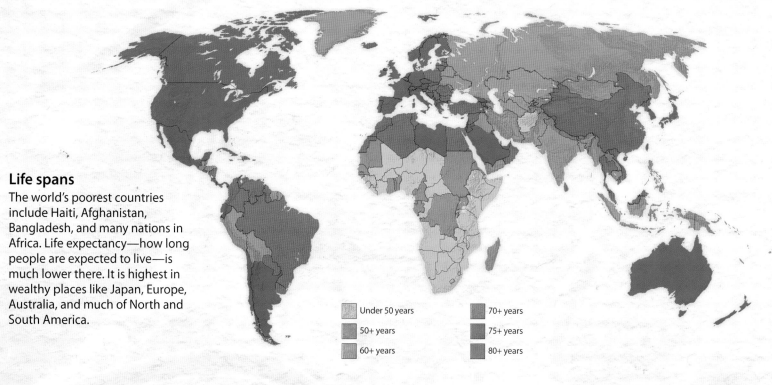

Life spans

The world's poorest countries include Haiti, Afghanistan, Bangladesh, and many nations in Africa. Life expectancy—how long people are expected to live—is much lower there. It is highest in wealthy places like Japan, Europe, Australia, and much of North and South America.

Under 50 years

50+ years

60+ years

70+ years

75+ years

80+ years

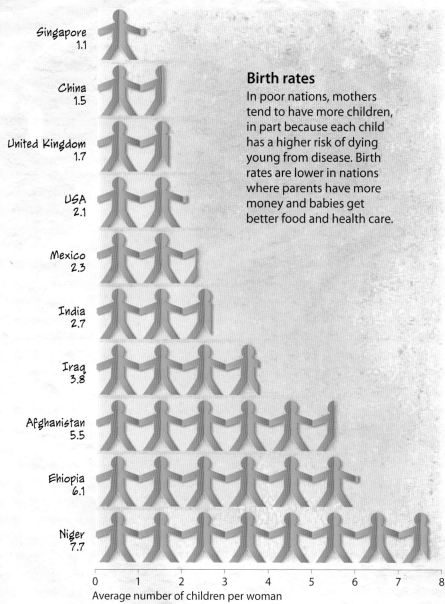

Singapore
1.1

China
1.5

United Kingdom
1.7

USA
2.1

Mexico
2.3

India
2.7

Iraq
3.8

Afghanistan
5.5

Ehiopia
6.1

Niger
7.7

0 1 2 3 4 5 6 7 8
Average number of children per woman

Birth rates

In poor nations, mothers tend to have more children, in part because each child has a higher risk of dying young from disease. Birth rates are lower in nations where parents have more money and babies get better food and health care.

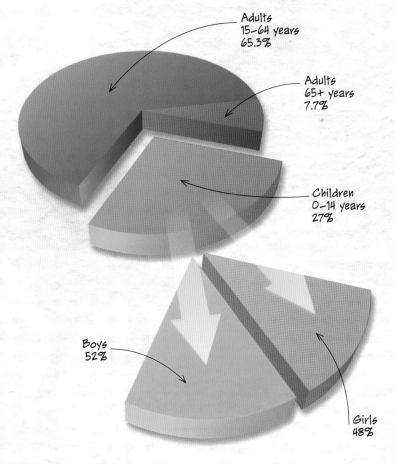

Adults
15–64 years
65.3%

Adults
65+ years
7.7%

Children
0–14 years
27%

Boys
52%

Girls
48%

Counting kids

Of every 100 people on Earth, about 27 are under the age of 15 years—that's about 1.4 billion kids! In general, a little more than half of the world's children are boys, and a little less than half are girls.

Amazing body facts

You are a combination of amazing structures and substances. Everyone's body contains trillions of delicate cells and one of the hardest materials on Earth—the enamel coating on your teeth. On the other hand, some features of your body make you different from every other person. Remarkably, your body parts do their jobs for a lifetime even though they are always changing.

Taller at daybreak

Did you know that you are about 0.4 in (1 cm) taller in the morning than when you go to bed? You get shorter because cartilage between the vertebrae of your spine becomes compressed during the day. The cartilage expands again while you sleep.

Ah-ah-choo!

A sneeze can force air out of your nose at up to 100 miles per hour (161 km/h). Most people's eyes close automatically during a sneeze. This reflex may prevent germs or irritating material in the nose from getting into your eyes.

Brain drain

Every day about 10,000 brain cells die ... but don't worry. You are born with about 100 billion brain cells, so there are plenty to keep the brain functioning.

Blind spot

Blind spot

The retina of your eye contains cells that sense light. Their signals, from all over the retina, travel along nerves that meet on the back of the eyeball. This place is a "blind spot" because there are no light-sensing cells there.

Something smells!

Nearly 3 inches (8 cm) up inside your nose are about 40 million sensor cells that detect chemicals in air, which produce odors. In all, our smell sensors allow us to pinpoint about 10,000 different odors.

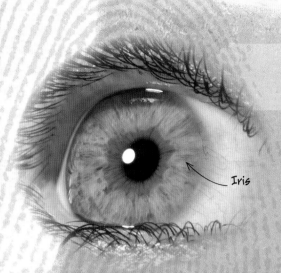

Fingerprints and eye spies

Your fingerprints and the iris of each eye are unique—one of a kind. This is because both are like puzzles, with pieces that can fit together in billions of ways as the body forms. A fingerprint has about 40 different parts but the iris has more than 266 different features.

Iris

Iris scanning
Like a fingerprint match, an iris scanner can be used to confirm someone's identity.

Super tooth enamel

The enamel coating of your teeth is built of calcium and other minerals. It is the hardest material in your body—harder even than your bones. The only substance that is harder than tooth enamel is the form of pure carbon that we call diamonds.

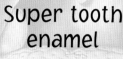

Flaking skin

Give me some skin

Your skin is one of your most amazing body parts. To begin with, human skin contains about 2.5 million sweat glands. Skin gets larger as you grow, so when you are an adult your skin will cover about 27 square feet (2.5 m^2). The skin also "recycles" about every six weeks.

Baby bonus bones

A baby is born with about 300 bones. As a newborn grows, some of the bones fuse, or grow together. Examples are several of the bones that form an infant's skull. The fusing of bones is why an adult's skeleton has only 206 bones.

Four bones at the front of a baby's skull eventually fuse, or join.

Breaking a sweat
Sweat glands are nearly everywhere on your body and help to keep it from overheating.

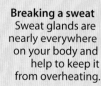

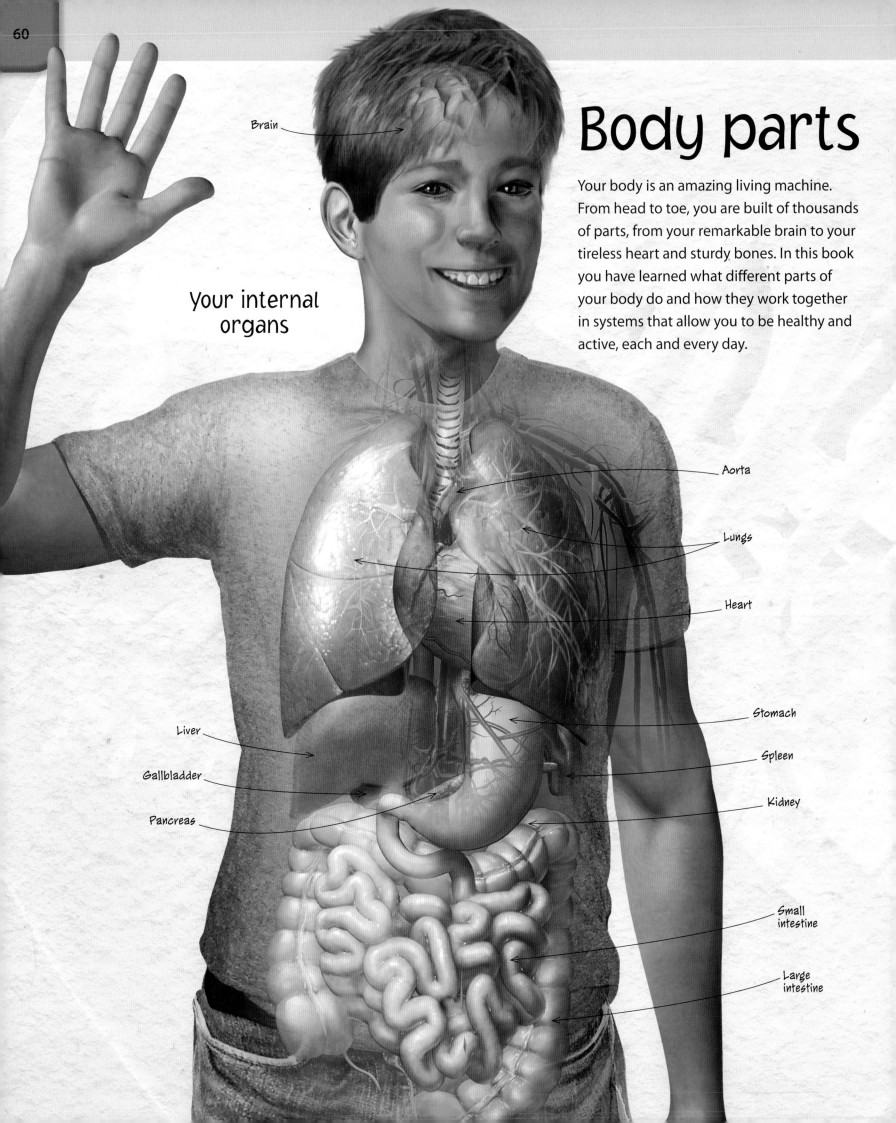

Body parts

Your body is an amazing living machine. From head to toe, you are built of thousands of parts, from your remarkable brain to your tireless heart and sturdy bones. In this book you have learned what different parts of your body do and how they work together in systems that allow you to be healthy and active, each and every day.

Your internal organs

Brain

Aorta

Lungs

Heart

Stomach

Liver

Spleen

Gallbladder

Kidney

Pancreas

Small intestine

Large intestine

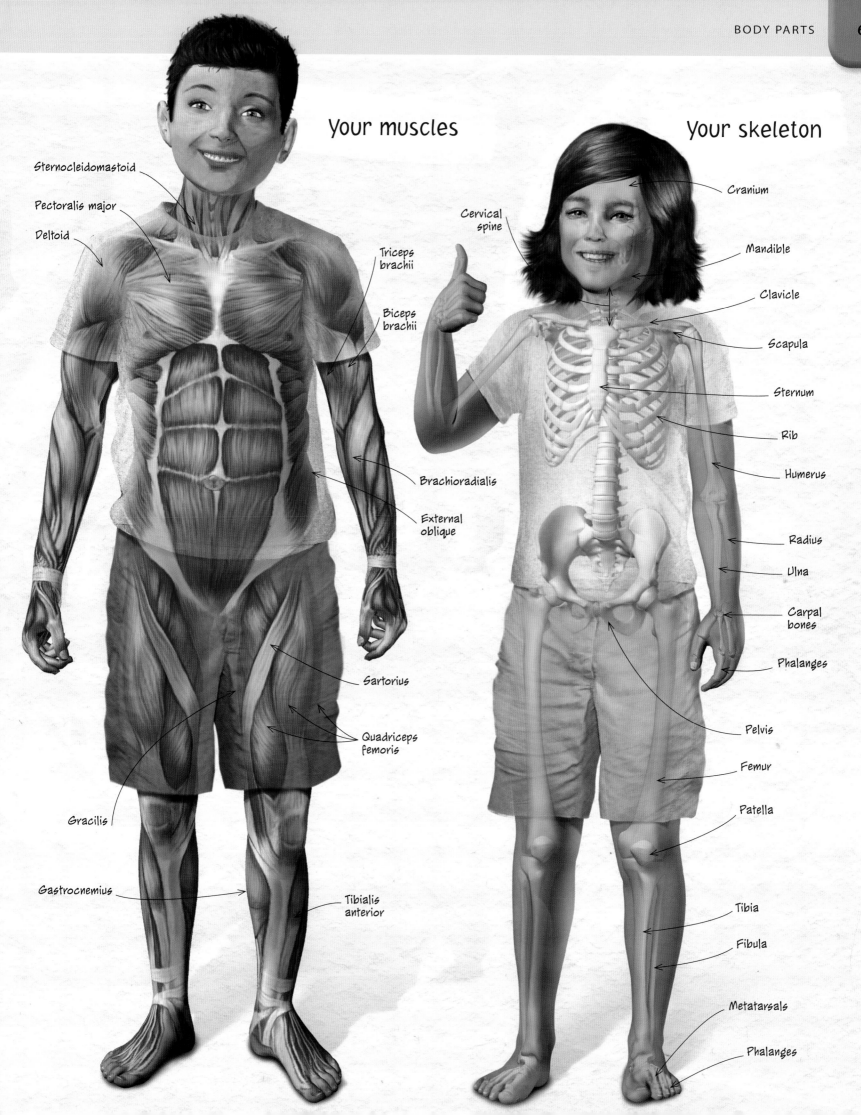

Your muscles

Your skeleton

Sternocleidomastoid

Pectoralis major

Deltoid

Triceps
brachii

Biceps
brachii

Brachioradialis

External
oblique

Sartorius

Quadriceps
femoris

Gracilis

Gastrocnemius

Tibialis
anterior

Cervical
spine

Cranium

Mandible

Clavicle

Scapula

Sternum

Rib

Humerus

Radius

Ulna

Carpal
bones

Phalanges

Pelvis

Femur

Patella

Tibia

Fibula

Metatarsals

Phalanges

Glossary

allergy A defense response in the body against something that is not usually harmful.

antibiotic A medicine to kill bacteria or other organisms that cause an infection.

aorta The largest artery in the body; it receives blood that is pumped out by the heart under high pressure.

artery A large blood vessel that carries blood from the heart to body tissues.

axon A long extension of a nerve cell that carries messages between neurons or between neurons and muscles or glands.

bacteria Tiny single cells. Some kinds of bacteria cause diseases; others are harmless to humans.

bone marrow Soft tissue inside some bones, such as the thighbone and the breastbone (sternum). Blood cells begin to develop in bone marrow.

bone tissue The type of connective tissue that fills with minerals and forms bones.

calories (or kilojoules) The units for measuring energy use in the body. 1 calorie = 4.2 kilojoules

capillary The smallest type of blood vessel. Capillaries bring substances in blood to each living cell in the body.

carbohydrates One of the basic types of nutrients. The body uses carbohydrates as a major source of energy.

cardiac muscle The type of muscle found in the heart.

cell The smallest living unit. There are trillions of cells in the human body.

central nervous system The brain and spinal cord.

cerebellum The rear portion of the brain, which controls reflexes that maintain body posture and adjust limb movements.

cerebrum The largest and most developed part of the brain, where thinking, planning, and learning take place. The cerebrum is divided into right and left hemispheres.

chromosome A structure containing a portion of the body's DNA, plus some proteins. The DNA of chromosomes forms genes.

chyme The mixture of swallowed food and stomach fluid that passes from the stomach into the small intestine.

cochlea The part of the inner ear where sound waves are converted into nerve impulses that travel to the brain.

connective tissue Any of the tissues, like bones and cartilage, that support body organs and other structures.

dendrite A short extension of a nerve cell (or neuron) that receives signals from other nerve cells.

dermis The inner layer of skin, beneath the epidermis.

digestion Processes that release nutrients from food.

DNA Deoxyribonucleic acid, which is the substance that forms genes.

endocrine gland A gland that produces hormones. The pituitary, thyroid, and adrenals are examples of endocrine glands.

enzyme A protein that speeds up chemical reactions.

epidermis The outer layer of the skin.

epithelium The type of tissue that lines internal and external body surfaces. Skin and mucous membranes are examples of epithelium.

genes Segments of DNA that carry instructions for building and operating the body.

gland An organ, or cluster of cells, that releases one or more substances, such as hormones, sweat, or tears.

heredity Receiving body characteristics from your parents. Genes carry the instructions of heredity.

hormone A substance made by some parts of the endocrine system. Hormones travel through the blood to target cells.

hypothalamus A structure at the base of the brain that makes many hormones and also helps to regulate body temperature, appetite, and other processes.

inflammation A general bodily response to an infection or irritating substance.

joint The place where two bones come together.

larynx The upper part of the windpipe (trachea). It contains the voice box.

ligament A band of strong connective tissue that helps to hold bones together in joints.

limbic system A group of brain parts that affects or controls emotions and memory.

lymph The clear fluid from tissues that enters vessels of the lymphatic system. Lymph carries microbes and other unwanted material into lymph nodes.

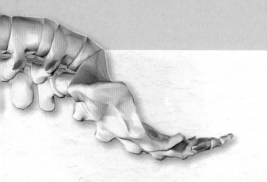

lymph node A small gland in which white blood cells destroy bacteria or other foreign material before they enter the blood. Lymph nodes usually occur in clusters in the neck, armpits, and other areas of the body.

lymphocyte White blood cell that takes part in immune responses. B cells and T cells are lymphocytes.

macrophage A type of large white blood cell that destroys harmful bacteria and disposes of other unwanted material.

melanin The pigment that gives color to the skin, hair, and nails.

metabolism The chemical reactions in which cells obtain and use energy.

mitochondria Cell organelles that make the cells' fuel. Cells contain many mitochondria.

nephron Any of the tiny looping structures in the kidneys that filters wastes and unneeded substances from the blood.

nerve A bundle of axons from several neurons (nerve cells).

neuron A nerve cell. The three types of neurons are motor neurons, sensory neurons, and interneurons, which occur only in the brain and spinal cord.

neurotransmitter A chemical signal released by a nerve cell's axon.

nucleus The cell organelle that contains DNA, which is organized in chromosomes.

nutrient A substance the body requires to function properly. Major groups of nutrients include carbohydrates, proteins, lipids (fats), and the nucleic acids from which DNA is made.

obesity The condition of having excess body fat. Obesity is harmful to health.

olfaction The sense of smell. The body's smell sensors are olfactory receptors that occur in patches in the upper nose.

organ A body part, such as the heart or brain, that consists of different kinds of tissues and has a particular function.

organelle Any of the cell sacs or compartments that have a particular function. The nucleus and mitochondria are examples of organelles.

pain The unpleasant sensation a person feels due to damage or irritation in some part of the body.

pathogen Something, like harmful bacteria and viruses, that causes disease.

peripheral nervous system The nerves running through all of the body except for the brain and spinal cord, which make up the central nervous system.

pharynx The throat.

pituitary gland An endocrine gland in the brain that works with the hypothalamus to manage a variety of bodily processes, such as growth.

platelets Cell fragments in blood that play an important role in blood clotting.

proteins Molecules that serve as building blocks, enzymes, chemical signals, and other key roles in the body. Proteins are made of chemicals called amino acids.

puberty The phase of life when a person's reproductive organs begin to function.

reflex An automatic response of the nervous system.

retina Tissue at the back of the eyeball that contains sensors for light. The

sensors are called photoreceptors.

semicircular canals The three fluid-filled canals in the inner ear that provide the sense of balance.

skeletal muscle The muscle tissue that attaches to bones and can move body parts.

smooth muscle The muscle tissue in the walls of internal organs.

sphincter A ring of muscle that can contract and relax to control the movement of substances through an opening.

synapse A small gap between nerve cells where signals from an axon cross to dendrites of a receiving cell.

tendon A strong band of connective tissue that attaches skeletal muscle to bone.

urine The body's fluid waste formed in the kidneys. Urine contains unneeded water and other waste products.

vaccination Procedure that introduces a vaccine into the body as a way to protect against some kinds of infections.

vein A blood vessel that carries blood back to the heart. The blood in veins has little oxygen in it.

virus A particle that can cause an infection.

X chromosome A chromosome with genes that cause an embryo to develop into a female if the embryo gets one X from each parent.

Y chromosome A chromosome with genes that cause an embryo to develop into a male.

Index

Credits

The publisher thanks Tricia Waters for the index.

ILLUSTRATIONS
Argosy Publishing Inc for all illustrations except the following:
Lionel Portier 51, food pyramid
Andrew Davies (Creative Communication) 56–57, maps and diagrams

PHOTOGRAPHS
Key t=top; b=bottom; c= center; l=left; r=right; tl=top left; tc=top center; tr=top right; bl=bottom left; bc=bottom center; br=bottom right; cl=center left; cr=center right; tcr = top center right; bcr = bottom center right; tcl = top center left; bcl = bottom center left

Agencies ALA = Alamy, CBT = Corbis, iS = iStockphoto.com, GI = Getty Images, SH = Shutterstock.com, SPL = Science Photo Library, TPL = Photolibrary.com

6 SH; **8** tr, tcr SPL; **10** cl, cbl, bl SH; **11** cr SH, t, tl SPL; **13** cr SPL; **14** cl, bl SPL; **15** tc SPL; **16** cl, bc SH, bcl GI; **19** tr, cr SPL, br CBT; **21** br TPL; **22** br CBT; **24** br SPL; **26** cl TPL; **27** c SPL; **29** bl, br SPL; **30** bl Sue Burk; **31** tl, tcl iS, tc CBT, cr TPL; **32** tc, c TPL; **33** br TPL; **34** br TPL; **36** cl, cr TPL; **37** t TPL, tr SPL; **39** tr, cr iS; **40** tr TPL, cr iS, bl SH; **45** tl, cl SPL; **46** SH; **48** tl iS, tc, cr SPL; **49** cl, tc, r, br, bcr SPL, tcr iS; **50** t, tl, cl, cbl, c iS, bl, br SH; **52** tl, c iS, bl SH; **53** tl, tc, tr, br iS, bl SH; **54** tr, cr, bl, bcr, cl, br SPL, c, bl iS; **55** tr TPL, cr, c SPL, br CBT, bc GI; **56** tl iS, tr CBT, bl ALA, bc TPL; **58** cr SPL, c TPL; **59** tl SH, cl, c SPL, br TPL

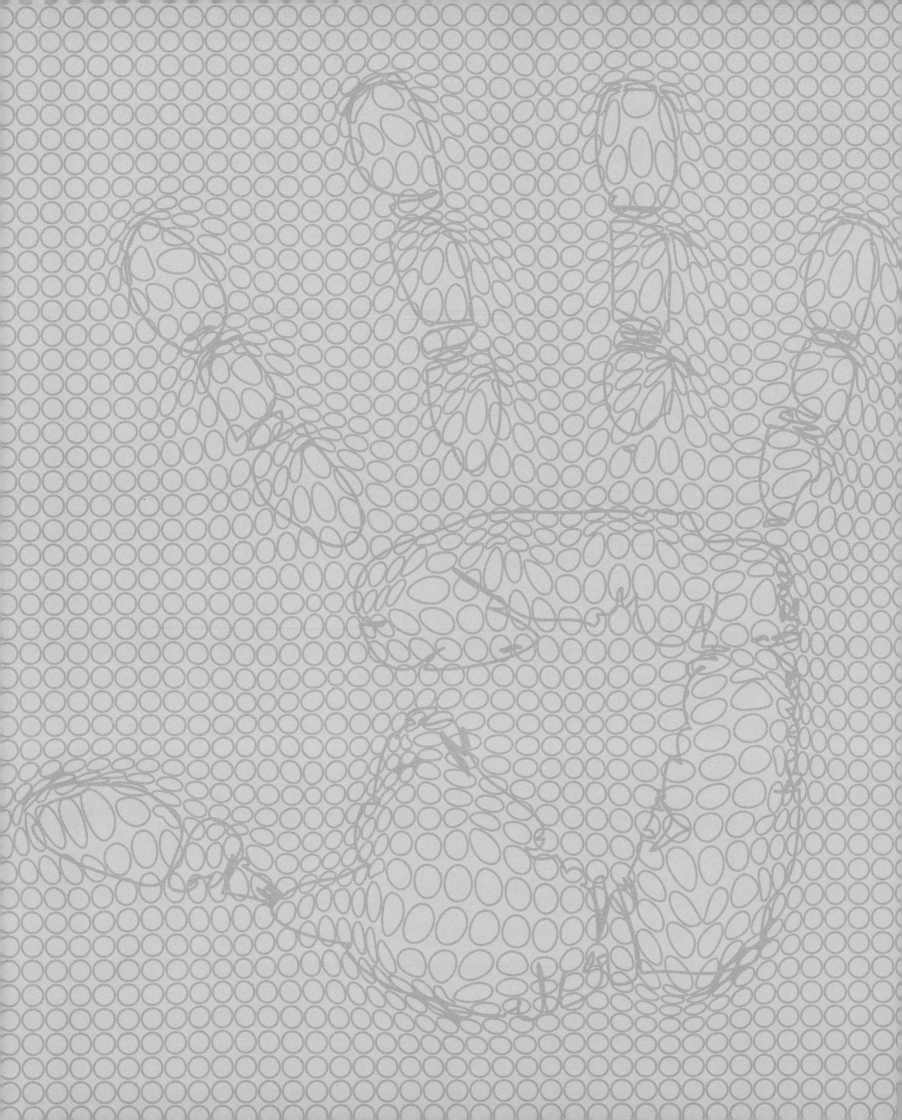